Moments
with God

Moments with God

Writers:
Jack Crabtree
Betsy Rossen Elliot
Karen Hill
Carole Newing Johnson
James R. Judge
Lawrence Kimbrough
James Long
Brian Shipman
Carol J. Smith
Randy Southern
Lynn Vanderzalm
Neil Wilson

Edited by:
Christopher D. Hudson

The scripture readings in this book have been taken from *God's Word,* copyright 1995 by God's Word to the Nations Bible Society. All rights reserved. Used by permission.

> *God's Word*™ SERIES and its associated logo are trademarks of God's Word to the Nations Bible Society.
>
> Up to 500 verses from *God's Word* may be quoted in any form (printed, written, visual, electronic, or audio) without written permission, provided that no more than half of any one book is quoted, and the verses quoted do not amount to more than 25% of the text of the work in which they are quoted. The designation (*God's Word*) must always appear after each quotation.
>
> Half-brackets (⌊ ⌋) enclose words that the translation team supplied because the context contains meaning that is not explicitly stated in the original language.

Developed and produced by The Livingstone Corporation. Project staff include: James Galvin and Christopher D. Hudson. Cover design by Paetzold Design. Interior composition by Design Corps.

ISBN 0529-10763-5

Library of Congress Catalog Card Number 97-60497

Published by: World Publishing, Inc.
                 Grand Rapids, Michigan 49418 U.S.A.
                 All rights reserved.

Printed in the United States of America

1 2 3 4 5 6 7 8 00 99 98 97

Introduction

*L*ife is filled with uncertainty. We hope to
live a long time, but we don't really know
how long we have. We hope to remain
healthy, but we can't completely control
our health. We hope to retire comfortably,
but we don't know what expenses are in
our future.

Thankfully, life is not completely
uncertain. God has allowed us to know the
most important person in our lives—him.
We can know who God is, what he thinks of
us, and what he will do for us.

Moments with God will help you discover
who God is. Each day's reading has a Bible
verse and a devotional reading that will
teach you about a characteristic of God.
Read a page each day, then spend the rest of
the day reflecting on the nature of God.

The Scripture reading from each day
comes from the clear and accurate GOD'S
WORD translation. The devotional readings
were written by people who, like you, want
to honor God with their lives. It's our
prayer that as you spend a few moments
with God each day, your faith, hope, and
love for him will grow.

Creative Genius

*Genesis 1:1,27—
In the beginning
God created
heaven and earth.
. . . So God
created humans in
his image. In the
image of God he
created them. He
created them male
and female.*

*E*ver stop and wonder at the
marvel of your own body: The
perfect harmony of billions of
cells keeping you alive and
functioning; the incredible
structure of your eye, which
allows you to enjoy a rainbow or
drive a car in city traffic; a brain
so complex it can store and
utilize thousands of bits of
information in a split second. But
even more marvelous is the fact
that the God who created you so
wonderfully complex created
you in *his* own image. Who you
are inside—your ability to love,
to forgive, to be kind—is a
reflection of his very character.
So if you—the creation—are so
amazing, what does that make
your Creator? Incredible!

A Moment with God

Praise God for
creating you. Thank
him for the wonder
of being made in
his image.

*For Further Reading:
Genesis 1:1-31*

1

Avoiding the Trap

*Genesis 4:7—
If you do well,
won't you be
accepted? But if
you don't do well,
sin is lying outside
your door ready to
attack. It wants to
control you, but
you must master it.*

A Moment with God

God provides for all your needs—physical and spiritual. Praise him for a love so complete.

*For Further Reading:
Genesis 4:1–5:32*

Sin is not a passive process. It is active, personal, and clever. Sin seeks to entrap and control us. The good news? The trap is avoidable. God has provided not only an escape but a way of overcoming sin. When Cain was angry enough to kill his brother, God lovingly warned Cain of the dangers that were ahead. God stepped into Cain's world in a way that could not be misunderstood and waved the red flag: "Danger lies ahead; change your course now!" God provided for Cain a way to escape sin, but the choice remained Cain's.

Thousands of years later, God works the same way. He's sure to give us an escape plan when we are tempted to sin.

Let It Rain

Genesis 8:1—
God remembered
Noah and all the
wild and domestic
animals with him
in the ship. So God
made a wind blow
over the earth, and
the water started
to go down.

When God judged the earth because of the wickedness of its inhabitants, the heavens opened at his command, unleashing a rainstorm of unimaginable severity. Yet when the Lord rescued Noah and the rest of the passengers on the ship, the waters could not harm them. All nature obeys God. Seasons change, plants grow, day turns to night—only because God allows it to happen. And when he stretches out his protective hand over his people, we can rest secure in his care. What can separate you from the power of God? Absolutely nothing.

A Moment with God

Consider the events that frighten or intimidate you. Praise God that he is more powerful than any of them, and he is able to protect you.

For Further Reading:
Genesis 8:1-22

3

The Sky Is Not the Limit

Genesis 9:14—
God said,
". . . I will put my
rainbow in the
clouds to be a sign
of my promise to
the earth."

A Moment with God

Think about a time when your skies were darkened by a painful episode. What promise of God did you hold on to?

For Further Reading:
Genesis 9:8-17

*T*he sight of a rainbow brings out the child in us, doesn't it? Just like a child, we want to share the sight with those around us. A rainbow is a lovely reminder of God's promise to never again destroy civilization by flood. Rainbows can remind us that God keeps his promises.

Whether we face dark clouds of pain, murky clouds of fear, or threatening clouds of loneliness, we can look to God. He protects his children even when we don't sense his presence. He remains near, just as he promised.

Divine Planner

JANUARY 5

*Genesis 12:3—
I will bless those
who bless you, and
whoever curses
you, I will curse.
Through you every
family on earth
will be blessed.*

*H*ow does God relate to the world in which you live? Do you picture God watching the spinning globe from a long way off? Or is God close and personal?

We don't know *how* God spoke to Abram, but the patriarch received an amazing divine promise: Leave home, and I will change the course of history. Abram had a little part to do. God did the rest.

God crafts a master plan. He can do whatever he wants. Yet, surprisingly, he chooses to work in and through us! God adds his unlimited power to our feeble efforts. God rarely tells us how he will keep his promises, but he asks us to trust him anyway.

A Moment with God

Take an important step of faith and set aside your desire to know how God will work. Simply declare your trust in God through prayer.

*For Further Reading:
Genesis 12:1-9*

How Could God Accept Us?

*Genesis 15:6—
Then Abram
believed the LORD,
and the LORD
regarded that faith
to be his approval
of Abram.*

A Moment with God

The best response to receiving a gift is to say "thank you." Thank God today for his undeserved gift.

*For Further Reading:
Genesis 15:1-6*

*E*xperience teaches that we are paid for what we do. We earn acceptance based on our performance. But God is not impressed by what we do because he does not offer his acceptance based on performance. That's comforting because we've all done things we're not proud of. Even if we manage to do good things, we often accomplish them with selfish motives. Left to ourselves, we wouldn't have any chance to please God. But the story of Abraham gives us hope. When Abraham believed God, God saved him. God is kind, merciful, and forgiving; therefore, we have the opportunity for salvation. Praise God for his generous gifts.

Nothing Is Impossible with God

JANUARY 7

*Genesis 18:14—
Is anything too
hard for the LORD?*

What are the impossibilities you face right now? Insurmountable financial pressure? Unrelenting illness? Uncertain future? A disintegrating relationship? No matter what it is, remember this: Nothing is too hard for God. His power is beyond our imagining. With just the power of his word he created the galaxies. With just the power of his word he created time and space. That same powerful God cares about you and all the difficulties you face. Instead of worrying about your stressful problems or assuming that nothing can help you, give your seemingly unsolvable problems to God. Trust him to do the impossible.

A Moment with God

God wants you to trust him to act on your behalf. Tell God about the difficult problems you face.

*For Further Reading:
Genesis 18:9-19*

A Heart for the Hopeless

*Genesis 21:17-18—
Don't be afraid!
God has heard the
boy crying from the
bushes. Come on,
help the boy up!
Take him by the
hand, because I'm
going to make him
into a great nation.*

A Moment with God

Ask God to show you someone in need. Take steps to show God's compassion to that person.

*For Further Reading:
Genesis 21:9-21*

After a family argument, Abraham threw Hagar and her son, Ishmael, out of the house. To any observer, the slave Hagar and her cast-off child were of no consequence. They had no family and no fortune. But God had compassion and did not abandon them. He provided for their needs, and he blessed the child. God hears the cry of the needy, and he is quick to take up the case of the outcast. Those whom our society rejects as worthless—criminals, the uneducated, the homeless—God values. He loves them as much as he loves you. They are not outside of his plan and his provision.

Immediate Answers

*Genesis 24:12—
Then he prayed,
"LORD, God of my
master Abraham,
make me success-
ful today. Show
your kindness to
Abraham."*

The larger the task, the more important it becomes to have an accurate assessment of our resources. Eliezar, Abraham's servant, proved he was well-trained in prayer. He prayed to God for guidance by the well in Aram because prayer was a habit for him. He was always depending on God.

Notice how Eliezar planned and prayed. He told God what he proposed to do. Through prayer, Eliezar allowed God veto power, and God clarified his steps. How many of our plans would take very different shape if we rehearsed them in prayer before we tried to put them into practice? We often miss God's guidance because we fail to ask for it.

A Moment with God

Even if your assignment for today isn't as unusual as Eliezar's, will you offer yourself in prayer as a servant for God? Ask him to guide you.

*For Further Reading:
Genesis 24:1-67*

Life Is But a Dream

*Genesis 28:15—
Remember, I am
with you and will
watch over you
wherever you go. I
will also bring you
back to this land
because I will not
leave you until I
do what I've
promised you.*

A Moment with God

God cares about
your troubles. Close
your eyes, be still,
pray to God, and let
his presence comfort
you.

*For Further Reading:
Genesis 28:10-22*

Jacob just had the worst day of his life. His plans for the future were crushed. His dreams were lost in an instant. An unexpected episode changed the course of his entire life. Deep in the night as he slept, God's presence comforted Jacob. The Lord gave Jacob a new dream for the future—one of hope and peace. Are you facing difficult times? Have your dreams died? Don't give up. God has wonderful plans for you, too. God is with you right now, offering you words of comfort, hope, and peace.

And in This Corner . . .

JANUARY 11

*Genesis 32:28—
The man said,
"Your name will
no longer be Jacob
but Israel [He
Struggles With
God], because you
have struggled
with God and with
men—and you
have won."*

*T*he reason for Jacob's name change was illustrated by an all-night wrestling match with God. Wrestling with God? The idea seems ludicrous—the mismatch of the century, to say the least. Yet Jacob probably wrestled with God throughout his life just like we do. While we don't wrestle physically with God, we ask the same questions that Jacob undoubtedly asked: "Why did God allow this to happen?" or "When is God going to do something about that?" Amazingly, God does not seem to mind when we reverently wrestle with (or question) him. In fact, based on the biblical narrative, the Lord—in his perfect patience—seems to take pleasure in those who struggle to understand him and his will.

A Moment with God
Praise God for the fact that you can freely bring your concerns to him.

*For Further Reading:
Genesis 32:22-32*

Protection That Never Fails

*Genesis 39:21—
The LORD was with
him. The LORD
reached out to him
with his unchang-
ing love and gave
him protection.
The LORD also put
Joseph on good
terms with the
warden.*

A Moment with God

Reflect on a time
you needed God's
protection and he
answered your cry
for help.

*For Further Reading:
Genesis 39:7-23*

*I*t's a truth that echoes throughout the pages of Scripture: God
protects those who follow him.
God gives security to those who
honor him. This doesn't mean
that we won't ever face difficulties
in life—Joseph is certainly proof
of that! Rather, it means that God
is with us, even in the face of
problems. Just as he did with
Joseph, sometimes God allows us
to endure a stressful time—
perhaps to season us, to equip us,
to mature us for future challenges
he sees ahead. As the story of
Joseph reminds us, God does
what is right—and that means
protecting his children.

The Long Arm of the Lord

Genesis 44:16—
"Sir, what can we
say to you?" Judah
asked. "How else
can we explain it?
How can we prove
we're innocent?
God has uncov-
ered our guilt."

Years earlier, Joseph's brothers had sold him into slavery. They must have figured that, if they were going to get caught, it would have happened long ago. Each time their reflective, old father mentioned Joseph's name, maybe they wondered if their sin would be revealed. Perhaps they wondered if they would ever have to come clean or if one of the others would eventually crack. But God's justice—even if slow by our own standards—is always sure. Rest assured, his books will be cleared—either in this life or in the next. Sinning against him cannot go unpunished.

A Moment with God

God's justice demands a price be paid for sin. Confess your sin with gratitude to the one who's already paid for it.

For Further Reading:
Genesis 44:1-34

Valuable Inheritance

Genesis 49:26—
The blessings of
your father are
greater than the
blessings of the
oldest mountains
and the riches of
the ancient hills.

A Moment with God

Pray by name today for those whose lives you want to impact with God's truth. Consider your family, friends, neighbors, and coworkers.

For Further Reading: Genesis 49:1-33

Now an old man, Jacob gathered his children and grandchildren for some last words—the blessing. Years before, he had tricked his father Isaac into giving him the blessing that belonged to his older brother, Esau. Now, he was the one passing on truth and dreams to the next generation.

His actions offer us an important lesson: the knowledge of God must be deliberately passed from one generation to the next. Our children won't "pick up" faith; they must learn it through our intentional teaching and modeling. God intends our words and actions to be a priceless gift to our children.

Wanted: Unqualified Applicants

*Exodus 4:10,12—
Moses said to the
Lord, "Please,
Lord, I'm not a
good speaker. I've
never been a good
speaker, and I'm
not now . . . I
speak slowly, and I
become tongue-tied
easily."*

*D*o you ever feel inadequate for
the tasks God sets before you?
Are you ever tempted to give up—
or not even try? God often puts us
in situations for which we feel
woefully unqualified. And we often
can point to someone else who
could do the job better or more
efficiently than we can. However,
it is in just such situations that our
God is ready to step in and
provide the courage, the confidence, and the resources we need.
God never asks something of us
that he is not prepared to help us
accomplish.

A Moment with God

Thank God for the
challenges he sets
before you. Ask him
to provide the
strength and
resources you need.
Praise him when
you succeed.

*For Further Reading:
Exodus 4:1-12*

15

His Higher Ways

Exodus 6:1—Now you will see what I will do to Pharaoh. I will show him my power, and he will let my people go. I will show him my power, and he will throw them out of his country.

A Moment with God

Is there something going on in your life where you just can't see that God is involved? Ask him for the faith to believe that he can use this situation in your life for good.

For Further Reading: Exodus 5:1–7:13

Seeing is believing, they say. But do you know what? "They" are wrong. It is often the exact opposite. Believing must come in spite of not seeing. That is what faith is all about. In fact, the strongest faith comes when we are forced to believe the opposite of what we are seeing. When our personal tragedies and trials seem to contradict our faith in a loving, powerful God, we soon find ourselves joining with Moses' complaining chorus. "What's wrong with you, God? Do you not see or just not care?" It is then, when we find our faith's candle nearly extinguished, that he seems to come close and whisper in our ear, "Now you will see . . ." and our faith becomes sight.

Celebrate God's Goodness

Exodus 12:17—
You must celebrate
the Festival of
Unleavened Bread
. . . You must
celebrate this day.

*I*n the middle of life's routines, we often forget to take time to celebrate the good things God has done for us. But take a closer look. In what ways has God blessed you or your family in the past few months? How has he rescued someone you know from a deep discouragement? What new insight has brought you hope? What kindness has a friend—or even a stranger— shown to you? All of these experiences point to God's blessing in your life. The God who blessed his people in the midst of slavery reaches out to bless you as well.

A Moment with God

Praise God for rescuing his people from evil and showering us with good things.

For Further Reading:
Exodus 12:1-29

No Way Out!

Exodus 14:13-14—Moses answered the people, "Don't be afraid! Stand still, and see what the LORD will do to save you today. You will never see these Egyptians again. The LORD is fighting for you! So be still!"

A Moment with God

Think about this: every struggle you face is an opportunity for you to witness God's strength at work.

For Further Reading: Exodus 14:1-31

*T*hey were trapped. On one side was a huge army, closing in fast. On the other side was an ocean of despair. Logic and common sense said there was no way out. God, however, is not limited by circumstances. With his strength, he blew a wide path open through a once formidable obstacle. He rescued his children because he cared about them. Are you trapped in a desperate situation with seemingly no way out? Has the word *impossible* crossed your mind lately? Have you surrendered to your circumstances? God knows your situation, and he cares. You don't have to fight any more; the battle belongs to him.

Indisputable Claim

Exodus 20:2—
I am the LORD
your God, who
brought you out of
slavery in Egypt.

When God gave the ten commandments, he listed first a
simple and direct command:
"Never have any other god."

Every disobedience of this
first commandment begins with
people substituting themselves
for God. As created beings our
most basic response should be
to our creator. When we try to
reverse the role and choose
whom or what we will call our
creator, we have unwisely placed
ourselves in God's position. Only
God can be God. Any substitute
will fail.

A Moment with God

Ask God to increase
your passion to help
you guard his central
place in your life.

For Further Reading:
Exodus 20:1-21

The New Neighbor

JANUARY 20

Exodus 29:46—
They will know that
I am the LORD their
God. I brought
them out of Egypt
so that I might live
among them. I am
the LORD their God.

A Moment with God

What does it mean to you to have the Holy Spirit's presence in your life at all times? Thank God for the fact that he is always near, always available to you.

For Further Reading:
Exodus 29:1-46

What if God lived in your neighborhood? Better yet, what if the very creator of the universe occupied a house on your block just so he could be near you? How you would you feel, knowing he loved you so much that he wanted to be close to you? The Israelites enjoyed just such a situation when the Lord chose to dwell among them in the tent of meeting. God loved his people so much that he actually "moved into" the tent to live among them. Today God still lives with his people. Because of his boundless love, he sends his Holy Spirit to dwell with everyone who believes in his Son.

Second

(and Third and Fourth . . .)

Chances

Exodus 32:14—
So the LORD
reconsidered his
threat to destroy
his people.

*H*e could be called the God of Second Chances or, perhaps, the God of Fairness: the God who finds forgiveness an easy assignment and a welcome task. Over and over again the pattern would be repeated: The Israelites stumble, God becomes angry, Moses pleads his people's case, and God reconsiders his verdict. Not only does God set the example for "going the extra mile," his actions demonstrate that the extent of his fairness is endless. The Old Testament God of Second Chances is the God we know today. We stumble, God is disappointed, we plead our case, and God forgives.

A Moment with God

Is there a matter you need to settle with God? He would love nothing more than to give you a second chance.

For Further Reading:
Exodus 32:1-14

21

A Holy Day for a Holy God

Exodus 35:2—
You may work for
six days, but the
seventh day is a holy
day of worship, a
day when you don't
work. It is dedicated
to the LORD.

A Moment with God

Dedicate one whole
day of the week to
rest and worship.
Ask God to help you
focus the day's
activities and your
thoughts on him.

For Further Reading:
Exodus 35:1-3

Stop. Relax. Reflect. Those are
three actions we're not apt to
take. Our hectic society has
taught us not to stop or rest for a
moment. We rush from work to
dinner. We rush through dinner
to another evening activity.
Finally we plop into bed at the
end of the day—exhausted.

Though today's pace is
faster than ever, God reminds us
to stop and remember him. So
why take time out on the weekends to go to church? We don't
include church in our lives to
keep us busy on the weekends,
but to take a moment out of our
busy lives. We go to worship
God and remind ourselves that
the many things of this earth are
never more important than God.

A Promise Worth Its Salt

*Leviticus 2:13—
Also put salt on
each of your grain
offerings. The salt
of God's promise
must never be left
out of your grain
offerings. Put salt
on all your offerings.*

God used the often-mysterious imagery of Moses' Teachings to help his people know him through daily experience and to give them a way of passing on devotion to their children. So when he gave the word picture of salt to describe his promise with them, he was showing them that his promise was good for all time, sustained by his own faithfulness, power, and love. Just as salt preserves the freshness of food and prevents decay, God's promises maintain their purity without fault, without fail. They always have. They always will.

A Moment with God

Present your heart to God today as a pure and holy sacrifice, remembering that his promises to you are trustworthy.

*For Further Reading:
Leviticus 2:11-13*

Who Says?

*Leviticus 8:36—
So Aaron and his
sons did every-
thing the LORD
commanded
through Moses.*

**A Moment
with God**

God's way is still the
right way. As you
read the Bible, thank
God for giving you
everything you need
to understand how to
live a holy life.

*For Further Reading:
Leviticus 8:1-36*

*C*onventional wisdom teaches us
to question authority, to make our
own rules, and "do our own
thing." Some churches even
decide what is right and wrong by
majority vote rather than adher-
ing to what is written in the Bible.

As the Creator of this world
and the giver of life, God has
ultimate authority. Every human
scientific achievement has only
uncovered how God set up the
world. The clear, specific instructions God gave the children of
Israel through Moses were
designed to help them establish
attitudes and behaviors that would
bring fulfillment and enjoyment to
their life. God knows best what
will help us and what will harm us.

A God of No Regrets

*Leviticus 16:30—
On this day Aaron
will make peace
with the LORD to
make you clean.
Then you will be
clean from all
your sins in the
LORD's presence.*

God took the initiative to make peace with us. A holy God, without sin, found a way to make a relationship with us, an unholy people. A perfect God, with no regrets, sacrificed his Son to enjoy his relationship with us, a people with many regrets. An immaculate God, with no stain or blemish, reached out to embrace us, a blemished generation. A gracious God, with the blood of his Son, wiped clean the hearts of his often-unforgiving children. He forgives with no regret. And he never looks back.

A Moment with God

Focus on the brand-new-feeling, no-strings-attached forgiveness of God. Confess your sins to him freely, without hesitation.

*For Further Reading:
Leviticus 16:1-30*

Life-giving Laws

Leviticus 18:5—
Live by my
standards, and
obey my rules.
You will have life
through them.
I am the LORD.

A Moment with God

Praise God for his wise rules and standards. Do what you can to learn about God's wise laws for your life.

For Further Reading:
Leviticus 18:1-5

We don't always like rules and regulations. We think they confine us and restrict our freedom. More often than we would like to admit, we inwardly rebel against rules and laws because they seem to tie us down. But God tells us that his laws are the pathways to freedom. His laws lead to life. In his wisdom God has set standards and rules that protect us, that help us make good choices, and that show us how to live a full life. In his kindness he gives us strength to follow those laws and find the fulfillment he intends for us.

True Justice

*Leviticus 25:17—
Never take
advantage of each
other. Fear your
God, because I am
the LORD your God.*

*E*very time we rationalize sin we also diminish our view of God. A proper fear of God helps us have a proper view of sin. The temptation to take advantage of someone else relies on the belief that God won't see or won't care. To fear God means to understand that the Lord misses nothing.

When we deliberately take advantage of another person, we dishonor God. Our actions can be compared to those of spoiled children who by closing their eyes and putting their hands over their ears think they can disregard their parents' words. Parental punishment is no more than a brief taste of the terror we invite when we disregard God in our treatment of others.

A Moment with God

What difference would it make today if you dedicated each word and action toward others as an expression of honor to God?

*For Further Reading:
Leviticus 25:13-17*

The Bonus

*Leviticus 26:3—
This is what I will
do if you will live
by my laws and
carefully obey my
commands.*

**A Moment
with God**

Consider the fact that
faithful people are
doubly blessed. Not
only do they escape
the Lord's judgment,
they also receive his
blessings. Praise
God for his
goodness to you.

*For Further Reading:
Leviticus 26:1-39*

*F*rom a human standpoint, there
is no reason for God to bless
those who obey his commands.
In his holiness, God would be
perfectly justified in saying,
"Obey my commands or face my
judgment." He certainly does not
have to coax or bribe people to
live by his word. Yet God offers a
"bonus" to those who are faithful
to him. Because of his love, the
Lord often gives blessings such
as peace, a clear conscience, and
hope for the future to those who
live by his laws.

Trust the Pilot

Numbers 1:1-3—
The LORD spoke to
Moses . . . "Take a
census of the whole
community . . .
List every man by
name who is at
least 20 years old.
. . . Register
everyone in Israel
who is eligible for
military duty. List
them by divisions."

*E*ver watch a pilot prepare for take-off? She systematically goes through her checklist as she tests all aspects of the plane's operations. A successfully completed checklist means her passengers can fly with confidence, knowing that the flight instruments are in working order and that the pilot knows the status of the plane. Our God is a bit like that systematic pilot. There is order and significance to everything he does, from creating an orderly army out of millions of disorganized Israelites, to the way he brings variously gifted people into a church to meet the needs of the congregation. We need never doubt that God knows all the details of any situation we face and that he is in complete control.

A Moment with God

Praise God that he is in charge of every detail of your life. Nothing will happen to you today that catches God by suprise.

For Further Reading: Numbers 1:1-4, 17-19, 49-54

29

More than a Number

*Numbers 1:2—
Take a census of the
whole community of
Israel by families
and households. List
every man by name.*

A Moment with God

What problems in
your life seem too
insignificant to bring
to God? Tell God
about them today.

*For Further Reading:
Numbers 1:1-54*

The book of Numbers is filled with
the stories and lives of over a
million people. Sometimes we feel
so removed from their experience
that we forget that these names
represent real people who had real
homes, real jobs, and real families.
They experienced the same
human problems that we experience. But Numbers reminds us
that God cares for his people both
as a whole and individually. He's in
the business of meeting needs. He
can meet our needs and overcome
our troubles, just as he's met the
needs of his people throughout the
years. Praise God that the Bible
isn't a series of stories about a far
off land and a far off God. The
stories of these real people who
were cared for by their loving
God can be a great encouragement to you.

The God of the Over-whelmed

Numbers 11:15— If this is how you're going to treat me, why don't you just kill me? I can't face this trouble anymore.

*M*oses felt overwhelmed by the constant grumbling of the Israelites. So he cried out honestly to God, not trying to couch his frustration in eloquence or timidity. "Lord, I can't take it anymore!" A gentle response met Moses' cry of desperation. When an urgent plea reaches the ears of heaven, God goes into action. Just as God sincerely listened to the Israelite leader, God listens and responds to his children today. We may be so discouraged we think we're out of options, but God's solutions to our problems are limitless.

A Moment with God
Spend a moment with the God who listens. Share your concerns with him, trusting his response.

For Further Reading: Numbers 11:10-17

A Deadly Bite

*Numbers 21:8-9—
The LORD said to
Moses, "Make a
snake, and put it
on a pole. Anyone
who is bitten can
look at it and
live." So Moses
made a bronze
snake and put it
on a pole. People
looked at the
bronze snake after
they were bitten,
and they lived.*

A Moment with God

God's forgiveness
knows no limits. Ask
him now to forgive
you for those times
when you failed him.

*For Further Reading:
Numbers 21:4-9*

*T*he poisonous snakes were
everywhere. Many people did
not escape their bites. God, in
his love, gave the Israelites a
simple antidote: All they had to
do was look at the pole with the
bronze snake on it, and they
would live. We, too, have been
bitten—by sin. Sin's poison is
deadly, filling our hearts with
evil and making us guilty. What
can we do? God has given us a
simple antidote: the cross of
Jesus. At the foot of the cross,
underneath the cleansing blood
of Jesus, we will find forgiveness
for all of our sins. Just as the
Israelites were saved by believing God, obeying his word, and
looking to the bronze snake, so
we can be saved by believing
God, obeying his word, and
looking to the cross of Christ.

Don't Run the Red Light

FEBRUARY 2

*Numbers 22:32—
The Messenger of
the LORD asked
him, "Why have
you hit your donkey
three times like
this? I've come here
to stop you because
the trip you're
taking is evil."*

We seldom get into trouble without God trying to get our attention. When we start down the road toward dishonesty or immorality, God puts up a series of road signs to warn us about the trouble ahead. Sometimes he places a friend or even a stranger in our path to confront us with what is right and wrong. In our private moments, God's Spirit reminds us of a Bible truth learned long ago: God loves us so much that he will go to great lengths to warn us of impending disaster.

A Moment with God

Thank God for placing "danger ahead" signs in front of you. Ask him to help you recognize them and turn around before you crash and fall into deep trouble.

*For Further Reading:
Numbers 22:1-41*

I Promise

FEBRUARY 3

Numbers 30:2—
If a man makes a
vow to the LORD
that he will do
something or
swears an oath
that he won't do
something, he
must not break his
word. He must do
everything he said
he would do.

A Moment with God

Don't spend your time with God bogged down on regrets. Confess your unkept promises and thank him that he always keeps his.

For Further Reading:
Numbers 30:1-16

We make promises all the time: "I'll call you!" "We'll have lunch." "I promise to make your game next time, honey." "God, if you'll just help me, I promise to. . . . " Sometimes we keep our promises and sometimes we don't. God wants us to be people who keep our promises because we serve a God who always keeps *his* promises. He stands by his word. He always delivers what he guarantees. He always comes through. He will continue to do so whether the rain falls or the sun shines, whether the traffic is heavy or light, whether your supervisor comes in with a smile or a frown. God remains true to his word.

The One and Only

Numbers 33:52—
As you advance,
force out all the
people who live
there. Get rid of
all their stone and
metal idols, and
destroy all their
places of worship.

*J*ealousy can be born of selfishness, such as desiring your neighbor's car or begrudging your coworker's promotion. But jealousy can also be born of love, such as a spouse's jealousy against anything that rivals the loyalty of his wife or her husband. God's jealousy is like that—only infinitely more pure—because he alone can see how utterly helpless his people are without him. When he commanded them to demolish every trace of idolatry from the lands he was giving them, he wasn't afraid they might stumble across something better. He knew that he was the only God and that his provision was already everything they would ever need.

A Moment with God

Thank God that he is jealous for you. He is not willing to lose you to someone or something that cannot provide for you like he can.

For Further Reading:
Numbers 33:50-56

Tempered Justice

*Numbers 35:11-12—
Select certain cities
to be places of
refuge. Anyone who
unintentionally kills
another person may
run to them . . . So
anyone accused of
murder will not
have to die until he
has had a trial.*

A Moment with God

Think of a time
when you didn't get
the full punishment
you deserved.
Thank God that his
justice is tempered
by his mercy.

*For Further Reading:
Numbers 35:9-34*

When we think of God's justice, we usually think of the punishment he metes out to those who've sinned. But in God's designation of the cities of refuge we see a fuller picture of his justice—a justice that is tempered by his mercy. In an age when human retribution was swift and often violent, even if the "crime" was in reality an accident, God took care to provide cities of refuge for offenders in order to guarantee them a fair trial. God isn't just the God of victims; he is concerned for the welfare of everyone, even offenders. Though this may rankle when we are the ones who have been wronged, what relief it gives us when we ourselves are the ones who've committed an offense.

Holy Break

Deuteronomy 5:12— Observe the day of worship as a holy day. This is what the LORD your God has commanded you.

The first four commandments direct our relationship with God. Three of them spell out the extent of God's holiness. We are not to confuse or misuse God's identity, character, or name. The fourth commandment orders us to imitate God by making one day out of seven holy. Six days are dedicated to work, one to rest.

God's example in creation teaches some important lessons. Rest doesn't mean "collapse from exhaustion." God didn't "rest" because he was tired; he rested because he was satisfied with what he had done. We honor and obey God when we set apart time to reflect, worship, and rest in his presence.

A Moment with God

Prayerfully ask God to help you re-prioritize how you spend your day of rest.

For Further Reading: Deuteronomy 5:12-15 (see also Exodus 20:8-11)

The One and Only

*Deuteronomy 6:4—
Listen, Israel: The
LORD is our God.
The LORD is the
only God.*

*T*he fact that the Lord is the only
God provided security to the
Israelites that their idol-worship-
ing neighbors lacked. The "gods"
of the ancient Middle East were
rarely thought to act in harmony.
As a result, the pagan worshiper
could never be sure that his or
her god was powerful enough to
fight other deities. The Israelites,
children of the only God, had no
such reason for concern.

This same assurance is ours
today. We often worry that God
won't be able to handle our
money troubles, health concerns,
or relationship difficutlies. But we
have no reason to doubt the
power of God. The Lord is
absolutely unique.

A Moment with God

What priority does
the one and only
God deserve in your
life? Talk to him
about his impor-
tance to you.

*For Further Reading:
Deuteronomy 6:1-25*

38

A Generous Repayment Plan

FEBRUARY 8

*Deuteronomy 15:8—
Be generous to
these poor people,
and freely lend
them as much as
they need. Never
be hard-hearted
and tight-fisted
with them.*

Can we ever repay our parents for all they do—for years of care and protection and love? Is it possible to repay the teachers who give so deeply? Is it even imaginable that we could repay God for his blessings? The answer is obvious. It's an impossible goal. No mortal could ever match the generosity of God. It is impossible for people to return the showers of blessings God sends. But God is honored when his children love each other. Perhaps that's why he reminds us to be generous to others. In doing so, our benevolent God is blessed.

A Moment with God

Consider the ways God has been generous to you. Have you thanked him today?

*For Further Reading:
Deuteronomy 15:1-11*

God Is on Your Side

Deuteronomy 20:4—
The LORD your God
is going with you.
He will fight for you
against your
enemies and give
you victory.

A Moment with God

Thank God for his faithfulness to remain by your side through the scariest of experiences. The Lord your God will fight for you.

For Further Reading:
Deuteronomy 20:1-4

What makes you afraid? What sends you into a panic? An encounter with a grouchy neighbor? An appointment that you dread? A client who is unreasonable? A persistent illness? Whatever enemies you face, you don't have to be afraid. Take heart. Don't be discouraged, and don't be alarmed. Remember that God is on your side. The Lord your God is fighting for you. The God who wins battles against the strongest armies in the world fights for you. He knows your enemy better than you do, and he will use his power to help you win your battles.

The Opportunity of Hard Times

*L*ife couldn't get any worse for the Israelites. When it seemed that God had abandoned them, they cried out to him in desperation. There was nothing wrong with God's hearing. He was ready and able to free them from their oppressors and mold them into a mighty nation.

Sometimes God uses our hard times to change us into the people he wants us to be. In those hard times God intervenes to help us learn new lessons and greater trust. Without challenges that humble us, we never learn how much God is willing to be involved in our lives. He wants to help us change our defeats into victories.

FEBRUARY 10

Deuteronomy 26:7-8a—
We cried out to the LORD God of our ancestors, and he heard us. He saw our misery, suffering, and oppression. Then the LORD used his mighty hand and powerful arm to bring us out of Egypt.

A Moment with God

Are burdens and pressures crushing you? Thank God for this opportunity to experience his work in your life.

For Further Reading: Deuteronomy 26:1-10

Forbidden Temples

*Deuteronomy 28:14—
Do everything I'm commanding you today. Never worship other gods or serve them.*

A Moment with God

Express to God his importance to you. Confess to him anything you have trusted more than you've trusted him.

*For Further Reading:
Deuteronomy 28:1-14*

God sees the temples of the modern world: shopping malls, car dealerships, and corporate ladders. He sees the things we trust and worship, and he asks us to remember to whom we belong. With righteous jealousy he demands clear ownership of our lives. With passionate love he claims us. And with fervent possessiveness he protects our relationships with him. He is right to want our full attention. He is the one, true God who provides and protects. He expects from us total faithfulness because that is what he has already given.

42

God Leads the Way

Deuteronomy 31:8—
The LORD is the one who is going ahead of you. He will be with you. He won't abandon you or leave you. So don't be afraid or terrified.

*R*elocating to a new town, entering the work force after a decade of raising children, pulling up roots to head for the mission field—all of us face at least one big move or change in our life that makes us feel uncertain, stressed out, and afraid. But God has promised that not only is he *with* us through such changes but he *goes before* us, preparing the way. Nothing that happens to us will take him by surprise or catch him unprepared. We need not be afraid. Our ever-faithful God is leading the way!

A Moment with God

Reflect on a time when a change in your life had you feeling uncertain or afraid. Thank God for being with you in that situation.

For Further Reading: Deuteronomy 31:1-8

God Is with Us

Joshua 1:9—
"I have com-
manded you, 'Be
strong and
courageous! Don't
tremble or be
terrified, because
the LORD your God
is with you
wherever you go.' "

A Moment with God

Reflect on God's promise to be with you in the midst of any challenge or trial. Thank him for being there as the source of your courage and strength.

For Further Reading:
Joshua 1:1-9

The Israelites stood trembling and fearful on the far side of the river Jordan. A painful forty years of testing in the wilderness was coming to a close. The future lay within their view. But Moses, the man who had consistently held their hand, would not be crossing over with them. The call of God to be strong and courageous was ringing in their ears. From what could they draw the strength and courage required? God gave them the answer, the one source and one source only—his promised presence. He would be with them, wherever they went, whatever they faced. Being with them was all he promised, and it was enough: Enough for them and enough for us.

Holy Footwork

*Joshua 5:15—
The commander of
the LORD's army
said to Joshua,
"Take off your
sandals because
this place where
you are standing
is holy." So Joshua
did as he was told.*

*I*n Japan, you are often required to take off your shoes before entering someone's home. In a way, the home is a "holy" place, set apart by the Japanese for this custom. Holiness means just that: set apart. Something that is holy in the biblical sense is something that has been set apart by God for a particular purpose. When Joshua stood before the Lord, he was asked to remove his shoes because the place where he was standing was holy. Why was it holy? Because God was there, and it was the place where God set Joshua apart to do his will. At this moment you are on holy ground, too. It's holy because God is here with you. He is just as present with you as he was with Joshua.

A Moment with God

Reflect on God's holiness. Thank him that he has made you holy by setting you apart to do his will.

*For Further Reading:
Joshua 5:13—6:27*

45

Deceptive Appear-ances

*Joshua 9:14—
The men believed
the evidence they
were shown, but
they did not ask
the LORD about it.*

A Moment with God

Make a conscious
effort to prayerfully
include God in your
decision making
today.

*For Further Reading:
Joshua 9:1-27*

We must always depend on
God's guidance. If we try to obey
God solely on our perceptions
without requesting his oversight,
we will be deceived by what
looks acceptable. Generations
are sometimes saddled with the
effects of decisions that were
made without consulting God.

Joshua and the other leaders
acted hastily and unwisely
because they acted on their own.
They made a treaty that should
have prompted them to seek
God's approval. They tried to
gain God's approval for their
unwise choice rather than to ask
God to help them choose wisely.
Their cautious independence
turned out to be disobedience.

I Promise

Joshua 14:10—
So look at me. The
Lord has kept me
alive as he
promised. It's been
45 years since
Israel wandered in
the desert when
the LORD made
this promise to
Moses. So now
look at me today.
I'm 85 years old.

As one of two spies who gave a faithful report to the Israelites concerning the promised land, Caleb had received two divine promises: One, his life would be prolonged, and two, he would inherit the territory he had explored near Hebron. Forty-five years later, Caleb was still alive. Though he had not yet received his inheritance, Caleb recognized that it was simply a matter of time because God keeps all his promises. God's faithfulness extends to us today: If we believe in the Lord Jesus Christ, we will be saved; God's Spirit will dwell with every believer; Christ will return one day and will reign in glory for eternity. All of these promises are assured because God is faithful.

A Moment with God

List as many of God's promises from the Bible that you can think of. Praise him that we can rest assured that all of them have been or will be fulfilled.

For Further Reading:
Joshua 14:6-15

47

Run to Find Refuge

FEBRUARY 17

Joshua 20:2—
Tell the people of
Israel, "Now choose
for yourselves the
cities of refuge
about which I
spoke to you
through Moses."

A Moment with God

Have you sought refuge? How was the God of Peace faithful to his promise?

For Further Reading:
Joshua 20:1-9

The God of Peace is also the God of Promises. He was determined to fulfill the pledge of peace he had made to his people, so he designated whole cities known as "cities of refuge"—places where those in trouble could find protection from harm. People in trouble could run to a city of refuge, assured that they would not be harmed. We don't have cities of refuge today, but the God of peace stands ready to insulate us with "peace on every side." Chased by failure? Hounded by discouragement? Pursued by problems? The God of peace is on the alert. He is our city of refuge.

Testing, Testing

FEBRUARY 18

*Judges 3:4—
These nations were
left to test the
Israelites, to find
out if they would
obey the commands
the Lord had given
their ancestors
through Moses.*

God is love. Sometimes that love shows itself as grandfatherly comfort, like an arm around your shoulder or a hand to help you up. But God's purpose is not to spoil and indulge his children, there's a side of his love that has a hard, tough edge—a love that can even use difficulties in our lives to back us onto a cliff of decision, to help us prove that what we say with our mouths is what we believe in our hearts. His discipline is brave enough to let us grow through the consequences of our actions.

A Moment with God

It takes both sun and rain to make a plant grow. Ask God to use both good and hard times to help you grow.

*For Further Reading:
Judges 2:11–3:6*

No Excuses!

*Judges 6:15—
Gideon said to
him, "Excuse me,
sir! How can I
rescue Israel?
Look at my whole
family. It's the
weakest one in
Manasseh. And
me? I'm the least
important member
of my family."*

A Moment
with God

What in your
background have
you felt limits your
usefulness to God?
Confess this excuse
to God.

*For Further Reading:
Judges 6:11-16;
7:9-22*

*D*o you have to come from a
well-known family, be indepen-
dently wealthy, or have a Ph.D.
to be used by God? No. If such
were the case, thousands of
names would be struck from
Christian history. Throughout
the ages, God used those who
were weak, poor, uneducated,
and unremarkable to do great
things for him. God is not limited
by the college degree you've
earned. His power is unfettered
by your social standing. When
you're tempted to make excuses
for why God can't use you in a
certain situation, remember this:
You, with all your limitations, are
the perfect showcase for the
world to see God's power in
action!

Settling the Score

Judges 9:56-57— So God paid back Abimelech for the evil he had done to his father when he killed his 70 brothers. God also paid back the men of Shechem for all their evil. So the curse of Jotham, son of Jerubbaal, came true.

*E*very day the news is filled with reports of repulsive deeds of evil—murder, abuse, fraud, and so on. Even more upsetting is the inconsistent justice given to those on trial for their crimes.

While criminals and evil doers often find loop holes in our justice system, there is one judge they cannot bribe or escape. God alone stands as the eternal judge—with the right and power to avenge the evildoers of this world. There will be justice for all those who harden their hearts toward him and continue to do evil.

No act of violence or evil escapes God's notice. We can trust God to avenge the crimes of our world in his appointed time and method.

A Moment with God

Equal to God's love and forgiveness is his holiness and justice. When you see injustice in this world, thank God for avenging the evil-doers of this world.

For Further Reading: Judges 9:22-57

When You've Done It

*Judges 15:18b-19—
So he called out to
the LORD and said,
"You have given
me this great
victory. But now
I'll die from thirst
and fall into the
power of godless
men." So God split
open the hollow
place at Lehi, and
water gushed out.*

A Moment with God

Talk to God about
your big dreams as
well as your specific
needs for today.

*For Further Reading:
Judges 15:15-20*

Samson had claimed a mighty
victory. Yet he had to ask God to
give him water so he would not
die of thirst. And God did it. He
gave Samson the strength he
needed for the fight and the
water he needed to rest. God
provides whatever we need, big
or small. God is always ready to
supply above and beyond what
we can imagine. What needs do
you have? What problems seem
to have no solutions? God is the
perfect provider. He knows
exactly what we need.

By Whose Standards?

Judges 17:6—
In those days
Israel didn't have
a king. Everyone
did whatever he
considered right.

*T*he lives of the Israelites at the time of the judges were characterized by these words: Everyone did whatever he or she considered right. Sound familiar? Our society has merely changed the words: If it feels good, do it. How foolish and arrogant of us. God's way is better. God knows what is good for us and reveals his wise plan for our lives through his commandments and his word. He doesn't want us to learn the hard way. He invites us to follow his ways and brings us into his embrace.

A Moment with God

Praise God for his wise plans for your life. Thank him that he shows you his will though his word.

For Further Reading:
Judges 17:1-13

Your God... My God

Ruth 1:16—
Ruth answered,
"Don't force me to
leave you. . . .
Wherever you go,
I will go, and
wherever you stay,
I will stay. Your
people will be my
people, and your
God will be my God."

A Moment with God

Let the variety of people you meet today cause you to thank God for the breadth of his love.

For Further Reading:
Ruth 1:1-18

Naomi practiced a highly unusual form of evangelism. She cut the legal and family ties between herself and Ruth only to discover that Ruth had become a believer in the one true God. The bonds that finally held them together were spiritual ones. Their friendship thrived on the basis of their mutual relationship with God.

The fact that God made himself known to a Moabite woman points to several crucial aspects of God's dealings with the world. He is Lord of all. His plan of salvation may have centered on the Jews, but even the family line of Jesus included people like Ruth. Her presence tells us there's room for us in God's love.

54

Saving Grace

*1 Samuel 2:1—
Hannah prayed
out loud, "My
heart finds joy in
the LORD. My head
is lifted to the
LORD. My mouth
mocks my enemies.
I rejoice because
you saved ₎me₎."*

*I*t's a mystery too wonderful to fathom. God cares so deeply for his people that he reached out to rescue them. In the case of Hannah, the mother of Samuel, the Lord rescued her from a lifetime of barrenness (which in ancient Israel meant no social status and a bleak future). Similarly, the Lord rescues us from crushing circumstances in our lives. More importantly, the Lord has provided eternal salvation for us through the sacrificial death of his Son. God's saving acts on our behalf are completely unearned; we have done—or can do—nothing to earn God's favor. The Lord's salvation springs from his merciful love for his people.

A Moment with God

Thank the Lord for the mercy he has shown you by providing you with eternal salvation—despite the fact that you have done nothing to deserve it.

*For Further Reading:
1 Samuel 2:1-11*

Utter Devotion

*1 Samuel 7:3—
Samuel told the
entire nation of
Israel, "If you are
returning to the
LORD wholeheart-
edly, get rid of the
foreign gods you
have, including
the statues of the
goddess Astarte.
Make a commit-
ment to the LORD.*

A Moment with God

Praise God for his devotion to his children. Contemplate what "total commitment" means.

*For Further Reading:
1 Samuel 7:2-6*

*T*otal commitment. Complete devotion. Undivided loyalty. That's the one non-negotiable request God makes of his children, that we worship the one true God. God is patient with us, but when our loyalties are divided, his patience wears thin. God forgives us, but when we worship other gods, he is not pleased. Do not worship other gods, he reminds. Not money, not work, not recreation—none of these should have a place in our lives if they take God's place in our hearts and lives, says the Father. God expects from his children no more than he has already given: a heart wholly devoted.

It's Never Too Late

1 Samuel 12:22—
For the sake of his
great name, the
LORD will not
abandon his people,
because the LORD
wants to make you
his people.

*H*ow often should we forgive someone who has wronged us? Many of us would like to think we would give a penitent person a second chance—if he or she were truly sorry. But should that person repeat the offense, most of us would wash our hands of him or her. God gave the Israelites a second chance— again and again and again. They failed him repeatedly and faced painful consequences as a result, but God was faithful and did not abandon them. God sticks with us, too, though we fail him often. He is bigger than any offense we might commit, and the importance of his plan for us outweighs the hurt of our disobedience. In his faithfulness, God is always there when we're ready to turn back to him.

A Moment with God

Reflect on a time when you failed God. Thank him for not abandoning you.

For Further Reading:
1 Samuel 12:6-25

No Other Way

FEBRUARY 27

1 Samuel 15:22—
Then Samuel said,
"Is the LORD as
delighted with
burnt offerings
and sacrifices as
he would be with
your obedience?
To follow instruc-
tions is better than
to sacrifice. To
obey is better than
sacrificing the fat
of rams."

A Moment with God

Praise God that his
desire for obedience
grows out of his
great love for us.
Thank him for loving
you so.

For Further Reading:
1 Samuel 15:17-30

*I*t's often easier to say "I'm
sorry" to God than it is to obey
all of his commands. But God
expects us to obey him because
obedience is how we show that
we truly follow and love God.
Full obedience demonstrates to
the world and ourselves where
our true loyalties lie. God
expects this obedience because
he is holy and perfect. When we
fully understand that he is holy
and lives with us, we cannot
intentionally sin. Yes, God is
forgiving. But God is also holy
and expects the same from us.

Inside Out

*1 Samuel 16:7—
But the LORD told
Samuel, "Don't
look at his
appearance. . . .
God does not see
as humans see.
Humans look at
outward appear-
ances, but the
LORD looks into the
heart."*

A résumé is one of two things:
either it is an accurate description of who we are or a deceptive
attempt to showcase who we
want someone to *think* we are.
Prospective employers have the
difficult task of trying to figure
out which is which. God, however, needs no résumés. He sees
the heart for what it is. He
knows our strengths, our
weaknesses, our goals, and our
fears. He knows our deepest
needs and wants. He can see
through the masks we may wear.
Only he knows what the future
holds for our lives. He knows us
better than we know ourselves.
And he still loves us.

A Moment with God

God knows what your
present and your
future have in store
for you. Trust him to
take care of you.

*For Further Reading:
1 Samuel 16:1-13*

The Secret of Success

*1 Samuel 18:14—
He was successful
in everything he
undertook because
the LORD was with
him.*

A Moment with God

You are not alone.
Thank God for his
personal love for you
and the success he is
bringing to you.

*For Further Reading:
1 Samuel 18:1-30*

*T*hose who describe God as
distant should talk to David. He
experienced the Lord's presence
with him in everything he did.
Throughout the early part of his
life, God's presence brought
success.

God loves to be closely
involved with the people he
created. He is a personal God,
capable of hearing our prayers at
all times and giving us the help
we need. God wants to be
intimately involved in all areas of
our lives so he can guide us to
do what pleases him. It has
always been his intention to be
our daily companion. Praise God
that we are never abandoned or
alone because he constantly
seeks to draw close to us.

When God Gets in the Way

*D*avid had a plan. He knew what he wanted to do. But through a sensible woman, God got in the way and changed David's plan. God's intervention kept David from sin. God is willing to frustrate us if it is in our best interests. He is a God who expects us to trust him even when our plans go awry. Just as a good parent steps in the way of a child's ball to keep the child from running into the street, so a good God intervenes in our schedules or business deals to keep us from harm.

MARCH 2

1 Samuel 25:26—The LORD has kept you from spilling innocent blood and from getting a victory by your own efforts. Now, sir, I solemnly swear . . . may your enemies and those who are trying to harm you end up like Nabal.

A Moment with God

Ask God for wisdom to recognize the frustrations in your life that provide direction from him.

For Further Reading: 1 Samuel 25:2-44

Lean on Me

*1 Samuel 30:6—
David was in
great distress
because the people
in their bitterness
said he should be
stoned. . . . (But
David found
strength in the
LORD his God.)*

A Moment with God

Don't expect life to
be fair. Instead count
on God's strength to
see you through to
the end.

*For Further Reading:
1 Samuel 30:1-31*

*L*onely. Confused. Misunderstood. Many miles away from God's promise of a throne in Israel, David found himself in the only place he could escape Saul's bloody sword—in the enemy's camp. This enemy had ransacked his home, stolen his family, and taken everything he owned. Now someone else wanted his head. But God's strength was enough for David, and it remains for us. It gives hope for tomorrow. It drowns out the sneers of those who oppose us. It emboldens the heart beaten down by awful circumstances. It is enough! God's strength is always enough.

Honor

*2 Samuel 2:5—
So David sent
messengers to the
people of Jabesh
Gilead. He said to
them, "May the
LORD bless you
because you
showed kindness to
your master Saul
by burying him."*

*T*he ill-fate of an enemy does not
give us an excuse for dishonoring them. The people of Jabesh
Gilead might have tried to gain
David's favor by treating Saul
and Jonathan's bodies disre-
spectfully. Instead, they carried
out their duties to their fallen
king with dignity. David understood that in honoring Saul, the
people of Jabesh Gilead were
honoring God, who had made
Saul king. For David, Saul's
appointment by God required
dignified treatment even in
defeat and death.

Long before David's descendant, Jesus, spoke the words of
God's heart, "Love your enemies, help them" (Luke 6:35),
David was already practicing the
principle. David understood
what God expected.

A Moment with God

It is no small thing
that God asks: will
you love me enough
to pray for and do
good to your
enemies?

*For Further Reading:
2 Samuel 1:17–2:7*

The God Who Guides

*2 Samuel 5:19—
David asked the
LORD, "Should I
attack the
Philistines? Will
you hand them
over to me?" The
LORD answered
David, "Attack! I
will certainly
hand the Philis-
tines over to you."*

A Moment with God

Think of a "battle" decision you face right now. Ask God to guide your decision-making process.

*For Further Reading:
2 Samuel 5:17-25*

There are a lot of books available on successful decision making, but we need only to look at the life of David to see the real "how-to" for making wise decisions. David had had some amazing battle successes up to this point, but he hadn't let them go to his head. Rather, he repeatedly consulted the Lord regarding what action to take. God's wise counsel is still there for the asking: who to marry, whether to accept a job offer or stay where you are, how to handle a difficult neighbor. Each "battle" decision you must make can be made successfully with God's guidance. There is confidence in knowing that our all-wise God is eager to give us counsel.

From Whence It Came

*2 Samuel 8:6—
David put troops
in the Aramean
kingdom of
Damascus, and
the Arameans
became his
subjects and paid
taxes [to him].
Everywhere David
went, the LORD
gave him victories.*

*I*t's one of the greatest rags-to-riches stories in all of history. David, a humble shepherd, became one of the greatest military leaders of the ancient world. The secret of David's phenomenal success? He recognized that every victory was given to him by the Lord. Without God's help, David was merely a sheep tender. What about us? Do we recognize God's provisions in our lives? Where would we be without the Lord's blessings? Our talents, our families, our careers, our achievements, and every other aspect of our lives are part of the Lord's provision for us.

A Moment with God

Consider all that the Lord has provided for you. Thank him for the abundance of blessings in your life.

*For Further Reading:
2 Samuel 8:1-18*

Principled Parent

*2 Samuel 12:9—
Why did you
despise my word by
doing what I
considered evil?
You had Uriah the
Hittite killed in
battle. You took his
wife as your wife.
You used the
Ammonites to kill
him.*

A Moment with God

Thank God for his discipline, for being like a loving father who corrects his children.

*For Further Reading:
2 Samuel 12:1-14*

"This is going to hurt me worse than it hurts you," many parents have stated this before disciplining an errant child. True as that may be, can you imagine the disapointment in heaven when one of God's children knowingly sins? Can you imagine God's disappointment when his children sin with the boldness of David? And yet, for the same reason parents discipline their children, God corrected David. Because he loves us, he insists on our obedience. He is a God not only to be loved but to be respected.

God Draws Us Close to Him

MARCH 8

*2 Samuel 14:14b—
But doesn't God
forgive a person?
He never plans to
keep a banished
person in exile.*

*D*o you ever feel estranged from God, as if he has banished you because you have done something unforgivable? Do you feel distant from God? We can take comfort in knowing that God is not like King David, who was unable to forgive his son and who refused to get close to him. When you sin and create distance between yourself and God, he wants you to confess your sin to him so that he can forgive you and draw you to him once again. Isn't it amazing that God—the king of the universe—wants to live in close relationship to you?

A Moment with God

Ask God to forgive you for things that create distance between you and God. Thank him for drawing you close to him.

*For Further Reading:
2 Samuel 14:1-22*

When Times Are Tough

2 Samuel 16:12—
Maybe the LORD
will see my misery
and turn his curse
into a blessing for
me today.

*D*avid was at an all time low: his son Absalom was trying to overthrow him as king and turn the people against him. But David knew God still loved him and believed that God could turn this miserable situation into something good.

God specializes in bringing good out of evil. In the middle of terrible circumstances, God helps those who love him find something good. God is compassionate and kind to us when we have hurts and needs. When our hearts are broken for a wayward family member, God shares our pain. When others abandon us or tell lies about us, God holds on to us and encourages us to move ahead positively with him. He never gives up on us.

A Moment with God

When circumstances and your outlook on life are at their worst, God is at his best.

For Further Reading:
2 Samuel 16:5-14

Something Better

2 Samuel 22:26-27—
⌊In dealing⌋ with
faithful people you
are faithful, with
innocent warriors
you are innocent,
with pure people
you are pure.
⌊In dealing⌋ with
devious people you
are clever.

God faces us as we are. We can't trick him into thinking that we are holier than we actually are. He responds to our faithfulness with his own faithfulness. He exposes our deception with his cleverness. He meets us with complete propriety. His reaching hand is always a hand we know and can grasp in our specific situation. God says *I am* what you need, at anytime, at any-place. And because *I am,* I will show you who you are, and I will call you to be something better.

A Moment with God

Ask God to reveal you to yourself . . . and then to make you more like him.

For Further Reading:
2 Samuel 22:17-37

And in Addition to That...

*1 Kings 3:13—
I'm also giving you
what you haven't
asked for—riches
and honor—so that
no other king will
be like you as long
as you live.*

A Moment with God

Thank God for all the good things he has done and for the many things he has yet to do.

*For Further Reading:
1 Kings 3:4-28*

*D*o you ever feel like you get less than you ask for? You go to a restaurant and eagerly order an item based on the mouth-watering picture in the menu, only to find out it is much smaller and less appealing than suggested. You order something from a catalog and find out that not all accessories are included and some assembly is required. It happens too many times. But it never happens with God. When God answers prayer, he not only grants your requests, but he often goes above and beyond what you asked for. He loves to be generous with his children.

The God Who Is Everywhere

MARCH 12

1 Kings 8:27—Does God really live on earth? If heaven itself, the highest heaven, cannot hold you, then how can this temple that I have built?

Can you think of anyone or anything that can be everywhere at once? Even the most powerful superhero in comic history could not be in more than one place at any given moment. Yet our God is able to do just that. He participates in thousands of worship services simultaneously, and he's there to give you comfort at the same instant he's on the other side of the world giving someone courage. The creator of time and space is not bound by time or space. He cannot be contained, used up, or watered down. He is fully there for each one of us every moment of the day.

A Moment with God

Reflect on God's omnipresence. Praise him for being uncontainable!

For Further Reading: 1 Kings 8:1-12, 27-29

All or None

*1 Kings 11:2—
They came from the
nations about
which the LORD had
said to the people of
Israel, "Never
intermarry with
them. They will
surely tempt you to
follow their gods."*

A Moment with God

God's jealousy flows
out of his love for us.
Reflect on what is
going on in your life
that could be making
God jealous today.

*For Further Reading:
1 Kings 11:1-13*

God is jealous for our affections.
This is not because he is some
petty deity with a need for
human attention, but because he
loves us so much. And loving us,
he knows it is only when we are
fully his that there is any real
hope for our happiness.
Solomon, the wisest man the
world had ever known, became a
fool. The core of his universe
shifted. Wife by wife, he slowly
but surely began to center his
life in a place other than God.
God knew that this shift was bad
for Solomon's life, his kingdom,
and his soul. The same is the
case for us. God insists on our
love. Not as much as for his own
sake as for our sake.

Deadly Detour

MARCH 14

*1 Kings 13:21—
The LORD also
called to the man
of God. He said,
"This is what the
LORD says: You
rebelled against
the words from the
LORD's mouth and
didn't obey the
command that the
LORD your God
gave you."*

We are never more vulnerable to failure than just after we have succeeded. God's prophet had a specific message to deliver. His orders included God's direction that he was to neither eat nor drink with the people of Israel while he was among them. After the message was delivered, the prophet lowered his guard on the way home.

On his way, someone invited him to dinner and convinced him that God wouldn't mind. The prophet believed a lie that directly contradicted what God had told him. The idea that God had changed his mind should have warned the prophet. Instead, he took a deadly detour. God called the act "rebellion." Those serving God are not exempt from total obedience.

A Moment with God

Ask God to help you exercise discernment whenever someone claiming to speak for God urges action which God has not permitted.

*For Further Reading:
1 Kings 13:1-32*

No Contest

*1 Kings 18:38-39—
So a fire from the
LORD fell down and
consumed the burnt
offering, wood,
stones, and dirt.
The fire even dried
up the water that
was in the trench.
All the people saw
it and immediately
bowed down to the
ground.*

A Moment with God

Consider the evidence of God's power that you see in creation. Praise the Lord that he is sovereign over all.

*For Further Reading:
1 Kings 18:1-45*

While God often works in mysterious ways, occasionally he makes himself known in wonderfully dramatic fashion. One such occasion was Elijah's "contest" with the prophets of Baal to see whose god would reveal himself with a sign of fire. The prophets of Baal danced themselves into a frenzy trying to get their god to respond—to no avail. Elijah prepared God's altar by flooding it with water. God responded by sending a fire that consumed not only the offering that Elijah had prepared but also the wood and stones of the altar—as well as the water and surrounding dirt. The Lord left no doubt as to whose power was supreme.

74

A Name That Means Evil

1 Kings 21:23—
Then the LORD also
spoke ⌊through
Elijah⌋ about
Jezebel: "The dogs
will eat Jezebel
inside the walls of
Jezreel."

*E*ven a God of love hates sin. Even the God of great grace cannot ignore blatant sin. And even the most patient God is angered by evil. If anyone ever tried God's patience, it was the evil queen Jezebel. She disregarded common decency, she thumbed her nose at the laws of God, and she dared to follow Satan. Enticed by sin, Jezebel personified evil—so much so that her name has evolved into a synonym for corruption. The despicable queen made quite a name for herself by willfully feeding her greedy desires, and her sin was rewarded with a death befitting her life.

A Moment with God

Greed is a destructive sin. Ask God to shield you from the temptation of greed.

For Further Reading:
1 Kings 21:1-23

Easy!

*2 Kings 3:17-18—
You will not see
wind or rain, but
this valley will be
filled with water.
You, your cattle,
and your other
animals will
drink. The LORD
considers that an
easy thing to do.*

A Moment with God

What is it you are
worried about? God
has more than
enough power to
handle your biggest
problem.

*For Further Reading:
2 Kings 3:4-27*

*I*f God didn't know us so well, he
might think we were crazy. He
watches us lay awake nights
worrying about bills to be paid,
deadlines to be met, guests to be
entertained. We worry rather
than trust the God who divided
the water so the children of
Israel could cross the Red Sea
on dry land. He's the one who
licked up Elijah's waterlogged
altar with a blast of holy fire out
of heaven. He brought the
Shunemite woman's dead son
back to life. Moreover, God's
power is so great, he considers
these wonders easy.

What keeps you awake at
night? What makes you feel
anxious? Rather than feel overwhelmed, present your problems
to your all-powerful God.

Promise Keeper

MARCH 18

2 Kings 10:10—
You can be sure
that the word of the
LORD spoken about
Ahab's family will
be fulfilled. The
LORD will do what
he said through his
servant Elijah.

*T*he best way to lose your credibil-
ity is not doing what you promised
to do. While broken promises
breed disapointment, a promise
from a dependable source builds
confidence and hope.

The Bible contains an
impressive record of promises
made and kept by God. Some
were fulfilled quickly; others
took many years for the results
to be seen; but none of the
promises made by God have
ever been broken. God is faithful
and true. We can count on him
to provide all that he promised in
the Bible: from our salvation and
eternal life to hearing our
prayers each day.

A Moment with God
Stand on the
promises of God
and you will never
lose your footing.
Praise God for his
steadfast promises
to you.

For Further Reading:
2 Kings 10:1-16

No Second Thoughts

*2 Kings 13:23—
But the LORD was
kind and merciful
to the Israelites
because of his
promise to
Abraham, Isaac,
and Jacob. He
didn't want to
destroy the
Israelites, and
even now he hasn't
turned away from
them.*

A Moment with God

Reflect on a promise
God has made to you.
Praise God for being a
promise keeper.

*For Further Reading:
2 Kings 13:1-6, 10-
11, 23*

Have you ever made a promise
you regretted later? Having
second thoughts about or trying
to get out of a promise is a
common human dilemma. But
our God has no such dilemma.
His promises are for keeps, no
matter how justified he would
seem in breaking them. When
God promised Abraham the
fatherhood of a great nation,
God kept that promise, even
though that nation repeatedly
rejected God and his laws.
Scripture is full of God's promises: promises to be with us
always, to give us his Holy Spirit,
not to test us beyond what we
are able to handle. How amazing
that such promises are valid
even when our actions prove we
don't deserve them!

God Will Not Settle For Less

MARCH 20

*2 Kings 17:40—
The people of Israel
had refused to
listen and made up
their own rules, as
they had done from
the beginning.*

*T*he children of Israel disappointed God many times. They made him angry. In fact, they made him furious! Why? Because they would not be wholehearted. They would not focus on God and only God as their master and provider. They thought God would settle for being one among many. And they were wrong. We have a God who demands our obedience and allegiance to him alone, to him above all else, to him no matter what. God will not settle for less, even if we do.

A Moment with God

Ask God to reveal the people and things that you put before him. Have the courage to accept what he reveals.

*For Further Reading:
2 Kings 17:13-17*

God—Our Guide and Companion

*2 Kings 18:6-7—
Hezekiah was
loyal to the LORD
and never turned
away from him.
He obeyed the
commands that
the LORD had
given through
Moses, so the LORD
was with him. He
succeeded in
everything he
tried.*

A Moment with God

Thank God for
choosing to be your
companion, to walk
alongside you and
guide you.

*For Further Reading:
2 Kings 18:1-12*

Just as God laid out instructions and commandments for King Hezekiah to follow, he promises to guide us. Throughout his word, God shows us the way he wants us to live—as parents, as neighbors, as coworkers, as husbands and as wives. And when we choose to follow his ways, he promises to be with us, just as he was with King Hezekiah. Think about it. God promises to be our companion, to walk with us through the joys and uncertainties of our daily lives. As our companion, he supports us, leads us, instructs us, and comforts us.

Point of No Return

*2 Kings 23:25—
No king before
Josiah had turned
to the LORD with
all his heart, soul,
and strength, as
directed in Moses'
Teachings. No
other ⌊king⌋ was
like Josiah.*

Josiah made his mark on history.
He was Judah's most godly king.
But he ruled a nation that was
under God's judgment. The king
instituted reforms in the spiritual
life of the nation, but there is little
evidence that the people themselves had a change of heart. In
spite of the king's efforts, the
national repentance, which would
have deflected God's judgment,
never materialized.

God judges nations as well
as persons. When a nation
comes under God's anger, the
just suffer along with the unjust.
Christians may suffer in the
process of making their faith
public, but better that than to
suffer later, knowing they might
have helped influence their
nation away from evil.

A Moment with God

Pray for Christian
leaders. Ask God to
show you opportuni-
ties for greater
involvement in
social issues.

*For Further Reading:
2 Kings 23:1-30*

Don't Forget

1 Chronicles 9:1b—
The Israelites were
taken away to
Babylon as
captives because
they had sinned.

A Moment with God

Consider some steps you might take to restore fellowship with the Lord when you feel forgotten or abandoned by him. Praise God that he cares enough to remember you.

For Further Reading:
1 Chronicles 9:1-44

*H*ave you ever felt abandoned by God? Perhaps you've felt separated from him because of sin in your life. Or perhaps you've felt forgotten by him in the middle of trouble or tragedy. The ancient Israelites certainly experienced such feelings. Because of their sin, God allowed his people to be taken captive. During their captivity, the Israelites felt abandoned by God and separated from him. Yet, through it all, God remembered his people and eventually restored them to their land. God wants to be close to those who love and seek him. No matter what the basis of your separation from God is, if your heart is repentant, he remembers you.

Fickle Faith

MARCH 24

*1 Chronicles 10:13—
So Saul died
because of his
unfaithfulness to
the LORD: He did
not obey the word
of the LORD. He
asked a medium to
request informa-
tion ⌊from a dead
person⌋*

*F*aithful to God? Or fond of the
world? Trust in the Lord of
lords? Or tempted by the lords
of humanity? Devoted to the
heavenly Father? Or dedicated
to the pleasures of life? God
expects one thing of his people:
complete trust and total faithfulness in good times or bad. Trust
me, he told Saul. Only when
things are going well, replied
Saul. Saul's faith was fickle—and
fleeting. When he became
fearful, he didn't talk to God.
When life got rocky, he sought
earthly answers. When the chips
were down, Saul went down, too.
Faithfulness: it's the one true
test of discipleship.

A Moment with God

Can you think of any
circumstance that
could pull you away
from God? Plan now
how faithful you'll be
when hard times
come your way.

*For Further Reading:
1 Chronicles 10:1-14*

Child's Play

1 Chronicles 17:20—
LORD, there is no
one like you, and
there is no other
god except you, as
we have heard
with our own ears.

A Moment with God

Reflect on the unique things God has done in your life. Thank him for each and every one.

For Further Reading:
1 Chronicles 17:1-27

*T*here's nothing quite like a brand new toy. We can play with it for hours, escaping from life's pressures and demands for the moment. Soon, though, every toy grows boring. Toys get old and fall apart. The fun disappears, and we are left looking for something else. What can fill our emptiness? The only lasting happiness comes from God because he is "new every morning." Only he can touch our deepest need and grant us real peace in the middle of life's struggles. God alone is capable of answering our prayers and offering us love and joy. Toys cannot hold us when we hurt, but God can.

Merciful Punishment

*I*t's human nature to try to avoid punishment . . . even if we deserve it. We shift the blame, make excuses, or argue about what actually happened in an effort to avoid the consequences of our actions. But King David knew better than to take such an approach with God. He had sinned by trusting in the size of his army instead of in God, and when faced with the consequences, he confessed and threw himself on God's mercy. He knew that no matter how severe God's punishment was, God was also merciful and would not give him the full measure he deserved. We, too, are spared by God's mercy. No matter how awful is our sin, God's punishment is tempered by his merciful love for us.

1 Chronicles 21:13— *"I'm in a desperate situation," David told Gad. "Please let me fall into the LORD's hands because he is extremely merciful. But don't let me fall into human hands."*

A Moment with God

Do you make excuses for your sin? Throw yourself before God's mercy.

For Further Reading: 1 Chronicles 21:1-30

The Owner's Manual

1 Chronicles 22:19—
So dedicate your
hearts and lives to
serving the LORD
your God.

A Moment with God

Consider God's intimate knowledge of your being—your needs and gifts, your pain and potential. Praise him that he knows you so wonderfully well.

For Further Reading:
1 Chronicles 22:2-19

How many owner's manuals do you have stashed away? The manuals contain not only instructions on what to do if something goes wrong but, more important, recommendations on what to do to keep things going right. Why do we view these manuals as an important source of information? Because we know that the person who manufactured the product probably knows what is best for its optimum function. It is the same with our Creator. He knows what we are best for and what is best for us. Serving him is what we are made for and dedicating our whole being toward that end will result in real and lasting fulfillment. This promise comes with a manufacturer's guarantee!

We Have No Secrets

MARCH 28

*1 Chronicles 28:9—
"And you, my son
Solomon, learn to
know your father's
God. Serve the
LORD wholeheart-
edly and willingly
because he
searches every
heart and
understands every
thought ⌊we have⌋.*

*T*he airport X-ray machine
checks your luggage for weap-
ons. An MRI examination
provides a vivid picture of your
internal organs, muscles, and
bones. What's next? A machine
that can read your mind?

We have no secrets from
God. He knows all about us—
motives, impurities, worries,
doubts—everything. If anybody
else had that kind of power, they
would either blackmail us or
reject us. But God knows all our
secret thoughts and still loves us.

Recognizing the power of
God to know us so intimately, we
have the freedom to be completely honest with him. His love
for us is truly unconditional.

A Moment with God

The God who knows
us best of all, loves
us most of all. Thank
God today for his
remarkable love.

*For Further Reading:
1 Chronicles 28:1-10*

When God Lavishes...

2 Chronicles 1:10—
Give me wisdom
and knowledge so
that I may lead
these people. After
all, who can judge
this great people of
yours?

A Moment with God

Lay aside your
agenda for now.
Approach God with
purity. Let him lavish
his delight upon you.

For Further Reading:
2 Chronicles 1:8-15

Solomon could have asked for
anything, but he asked for
wisdom to serve God well. His
priorities were in line. His
motivations were pure. And he
received not only the things for
which he asked, but also the
blessings for which he did not
ask. God lavished upon
Solomon's pure motivations
riches and honor because God
delighted in pure motives. God
revels in hearts that seek the
higher ground. God loves to give
to hearts committed to him
because he can trust those
hearts with good things.

God's Present Reality

MARCH 30

2 Chronicles 7:17-18a—
If you will be faithful to me as your father David was, do everything I command, and obey my laws and rules, then I will establish your royal dynasty.

*T*he glory of God is an elusive concept. How can you describe it? Can you sense it only by shivers and goosebumps, or is it often casually present in the throaty whistle of a songbird or the first flower of spring? Truly, God's glory—his splendor, his radiance, his brilliance, his creative touch—is everywhere, all the time. But there are moments, it seems, when he opens our spiritual eyes a little wider, when he stirs our hope for a day, when his glory is all we'll know. We may never find words for it, but yes, one day, we'll know. Oh, how we'll know!

A Moment with God

Spend enough time praying today to silence the noise of this world, and wait on God to reveal his glory.

For Further Reading:
2 Chronicles 7:1-22

You're Right!

2 Chronicles 12:5-6—
The prophet Shemaiah . . . said to them, "This is what the LORD says: You have abandoned me, so I will abandon you. . . ."
Then the commanders of Israel and the king humbled themselves. "The LORD is right!" they said.

A Moment With God

Consider the following prayer: "Lord, allow me to hear your corrections early, for I fear the results of my mistakes."

For Further Reading: 2 Chronicles 12:1-14

*F*ear can be a powerful encouragement toward repentance. Fear can also cause people to fake remorse. Sometimes we can't tell the difference in ourselves. Fortunately, God can always separate the false from the real thing.

With the army of Shishak beating on the door of Jerusalem, the prophet Shemaiah spoke God's judgment. The king and the leaders repented. God recognized the genuineness of their repentance. So God adjusted the consequences for their behavior. Instead of utter destruction, they suffered humiliating defeat.

Even when we realize our sin, we may still have to face the consequences of our disobedience.

24-7-365

*M*any models and techniques are used to teach Christians how to pray effectivly. One of the best known of these techniques is the ACTS model of prayer. An ACTS prayer includes *adoration* of God, *confession* of sin, *thanksgiving* for God's blessings, and *supplication* or requests for God's work. While the ACTS technique is certainly valuable, not every prayer situation lends itself to such a model. What about those times when a need arises so suddenly that you only cry, "Lord, please help me"? Good news: God responds to those prayers as well. In retail terms, God would be classified as a 24-7-365 outlet. He is "open" 24 hours a day, 7 days a week, 365 days a year. Put simply, God is always available.

APRIL 1

*2 Chronicles 14:11-12—
Asa called on the LORD his God. He said, "LORD, there is no one except you who can help those who are not strong so that they can fight against a large ₁army₁. Help us, LORD our God, because we are depending on you."*

A Moment with God

Think of the quickest answer to prayer you've ever received. Praise God for the fact that he is accessible to respond to immediate prayers.

For Further Reading: 2 Chronicles 14:2-15

Utterly Fair

2 Chronicles 19:4—While Jehoshaphat was living in Jerusalem, he regularly went to the people between Beersheba and the mountains of Ephraim. He brought the people back to the LORD God of their ancestors.

A Moment with God

Remember that God's judgments are just, even if you don't understand everything you see. Thank him for being incorruptible.

For Further Reading: 2 Chronicles 19:1-11

When you think of our judicial system, what comes to mind? The judge charged with taking bribes? The murderer released on a technicality? The creeds "innocent until proven guilty" or "justice is blind"—slogans that sound great but seem to be impossible to enforce? When you're tempted to be cynical about our flawed legal system, remember that there is an ultimate Judge who is incorruptible. The justice he delivers is truly impartial and utterly fair. His courtroom is the span of eternity, and he can't be bought, threatened, or cajoled out of judging rightly.

The Optimist

*2 Chronicles 24:19—
The LORD sent
them prophets to
bring them back to
himself. The
prophets warned
them, but they
wouldn't listen.*

What an optimist is our God! His people lived a history pockmarked by sin and disobedience. They were known for their rebellion, disunity, and disrespect for God and his laws. But one thing is hard for God to do: give up on his people! A pessimistic God would have looked upon the situation in Jerusalem and said, "Forget it—these people will never get it right!" But the God of hope provided still another opportunity for faith to grow among his children: He sent prophets to guide them back to him. That's what a hopeful God does for his children!

A Moment with God

When you feel that you disappointed God, remember that God hasn't given up on you.

*For Further Reading:
2 Chronicles 24:1-22*

You Have an Ally

*2 Chronicles 26:7—
God helped him
when he attacked
the Philistines, the
Arabs who lived in
Gur Baal, and the
Meunites.*

A Moment with God

Thank God that he
doesn't leave you
helpless against
your enemies. Praise
him for giving you
all you need to fight
the battles.

*For Further Reading:
2 Chronicles 26:1-23*

*D*o you have enemies? Maybe none like the ones the Israelites had. But do you find yourself fighting against inner enemies such as anger, arrogance, faithlessness, jealousy, impatience, a bitter spirit, or selfishness? God wants to help you. Just as he helped the Israelites fight against their fiercest enemies, he will help you fight against yours. God won't do all the fighting for you, but when he sees you gearing up to fight the enemies that threaten your spiritual life, he will eagerly fight with you. Through the power of his word and the Holy Spirit, God will give you everything you need to overcome your enemies.

Greater Than Expected

*2 Chronicles 30:9—
The LORD your
God is merciful
and compassion-
ate. He will not
turn his face away
from you if you
return to him.*

God's love stood the test. For hundreds of years the people of Israel were lured into worshiping idols and false gods instead of the living God who had rescued their ancestors from slavery in Egypt. While they were grossly unfaithful to God, he remained faithful to them. God was angered by their many sins and often warned them, then punished them. However, when they hit bottom and started looking for help, God's response to them was always full of mercy and compassion.

Is God a fool to be so ready to forgive? No, he has supernatural strength and deep love that keeps the doors open for people like us to come back to him.

A Moment with God

Mercy is kindness to a wrongdoer that is greater than might be expected. Thank God today that his love is greater than you ever expected or deserved it to be.

*For Further Reading:
2 Chronicles 30:1-9*

Look at Me When I Talk to You!

*2 Chronicles 33:10—
When the Lord
spoke to Manasseh
and his people,
they wouldn't even
pay attention.*

*I*t is God's desire to talk to his children. God speaks in many ways—through the Bible, through circumstances, through other people. And God demands to be heard. Often, as with Manasseh, he will speak louder and louder until he knows he has our attention. It is not enough for God to talk to his children while we work, watch TV, or read the newspaper and basically ignore him. He insists that we always listen and be ready to hear his voice at the first whisper, ready to respond at the first request.

A Moment with God

Don't let your prayer today be just asking God about something or telling him your problem. Take time to be quiet and listen.

*For Further Reading:
2 Chronicles 33:1-13*

One More Chance

*2 Chronicles 36:15—
The L ORD God of
their ancestors
repeatedly sent
messages through
his messengers
because he wanted
to spare his people
and his dwelling
place.*

*I*n baseball, you have three strikes before you are out. No more. When the third strike whizzes by, you return to the dugout, pondering your failure. Life often seems like a baseball game. You only have so many chances before you are labeled a failure. Thankfully, though, the Christian life is more like batting practice than like a baseball game. Your coach, the Lord, faithfully stands behind you, whispering instructions to improve your swing. Lean this way. Choke up on the bat. Keep your eye on the ball. He works with you until you succeed, no matter how many strikes it takes.

A Moment with God

Thank God for his limitless patience. Rest easy knowing that he is not finished with you yet.

*For Further Reading:
1 Chronicles 36:1-23*

Ownership

APRIL 8

Ezra 1:7—
King Cyrus brought
out the utensils
belonging to the
LORD's temple.
Nebuchadnezzar
had taken these
utensils from
Jerusalem and put
them in the temple
of his own god.

A Moment with God

If you haven't done it in a while, take a moment to acknowledge God's ownership of your life.

For Further Reading:
Ezra 1:1-11

God never loses track of what belongs to him. God allowed his people to be defeated and his temple to be sacked, but he remained in control. Nebuchadnezzar may have thought he was the new owner of God's things, but history proves God simply loaned him the temple utensils until the resettlement of the promised land under Ezra. Isaiah even recorded all these events in his prophecies 150 years before they occurred (Isaiah 44:28). God directs the history of the world.

Whether events occur on the world stage or in our backyard, God remains in control. He stays in touch with his creation, including us.

God Can't Be Under- mined

Ezra 5:5—
But the leaders of
the Jews were under
God's watchful eye.
They couldn't be
stopped until
Darius received a
report and sent a
reply to it.

*I*t's no surprise that when we do God's work, we become a prime target for Satan. He delights in frustrating, confusing, and sidetracking our efforts. Maybe you are trying to witness to a coworker and find that your discussions are always inter-rupted. Maybe, upon deciding to go to the mission field, you suddenly find yourself battling a prolonged illness. Whatever Satan's attack, you need not be afraid; God is in control. Nothing Satan throws in your path can thwart or undermine God's plan. God is Lord of every circum-stance; he can't be taken by surprise. His mastery over every situation is so complete that he can even use Satan's interrup-tions to further his purpose!

A Moment with God

Don't let Satan's attacks frustrate you. Reflect on God's control over every situation and praise him for it.

For Further Reading:
Ezra 5:1-5

Free Indeed

Ezra 7:28—
He made the king,
his advisers,
and all the king's
powerful officials
treat me kindly.
I was encouraged
because the LORD
my God was
guiding me. So I
gathered leaders in
Israel to go with me.

A Moment with God

God is in control, provident and present, always. Thank him that there is a pattern and order to our world even when we cannot see it.

For Further Reading:
Ezra 7:12-28

*E*ver wonder whether anyone really knows what is going on with this world? The Israelites must certainly have wondered this until out of nowhere there appeared evidence to the contrary. Their long captivity and slavery ended suddenly. They returned to Jerusalem to find the place of their worship destroyed. How could it ever be restored to a place that was worthy of their God? The question was answered in a moment as they remembered a long-forgotten promise tucked into history by a God who was always there. God remains with us, too. In the times that you feel like your life is spinning, you can remember that God remains with you and in firm control of your life.

The Joy of the Undeserving

W̶hat do you deserve from your family? Perhaps unconditional love and respect. What do you deserve from your friends? Perhaps to be treated in the same way that you treat them. What do you deserve from your boss, professors, or teachers? Perhaps fair compensation for your work. What do you deserve from God? Nothing more than eternal punishment. God is holy, and his holiness demands punishment for sin. However, because of his mercy, God chooses not to treat us as we deserve. Jesus bore God's entire punishment for our sins. As a result, those who believe in him will be able to spend eternity in the presence of the merciful God—an undeserved fate if ever there was one.

Ezra 9:13—
After all that has happened to us because of the evil things we have done and because of our overwhelming guilt, you, our God, have punished us far less than we deserve and have permitted a few of us to survive.

A Moment with God

Consider what would happen if God treated you as you deserve, based on the fact that you are a sinner. Thank him for his abundant mercy.

For Further Reading: Ezra 9:1-15

When God's People Pray

Nehemiah 1:11— Lord, please pay attention to my prayer and to the prayers of all your other servants who want to worship your name. Please give me success today and make this man, King Artaxerxes, show me compassion.

A Moment with God

Climb up in your heavenly Father's lap today and share your heart with him.

For Further Reading: Nehemiah 1:1-11

Nehemiah knew God well. He knew that God listens when his people pray. Like a father whose child climbs up in his lap to share a concern, God is blessed when his children cry out to him. Prayer acknowledges God's authority. Prayer affirms God's power. And prayer advocates action—godly action. So when Nehemiah insisted that God pay attention to his urgent plea, he knew God would care enough to listen. And he trusted God to do what is right. The God of prayer is blessed when his people pray.

The God Who Is with Us

Nehemiah 2:18—Then I told them that my God had been guiding me and what the king had told me. They replied, "Let's begin to rebuild." So they encouraged one another to begin this God-pleasing work.

Somehow, it seems easy to believe in God's majesty or his greatness. Those characteristics are just part of who he is. Even what we don't understand about them we accept as our own limitations, not his. But the truly unbelievable side of God's nature is that even from his position of splendor and supremacy he chooses to become involved in our lives. He daily takes an interest in where we are, what we're doing, who we're around. In ways we don't even see, he guides us through the circumstances of life because he loves us and cares for us.

A Moment with God

Feeling lost on your way to wherever you're going? Ask God to guide you, then trust that he is.

For Further Reading: Nehemiah 2:11-20

Focus on God

*Nehemiah 4:14—
I looked them over
and proceeded to
tell the nobles, the
leaders, and the
rest of the people,
"Don't be afraid of
our enemies.
Remember how
great and awe-
inspiring the
LORD is."*

A Moment with God

Consider all the "enemies" that oppose God's work in your life. Think about the power of God that is available to you. Thank God for giving you everything you need to do your job.

*For Further Reading:
Nehemiah 4:4-20*

Rebuilding the walls of Jerusalem before their enemies launched a deadly assault was a long shot for Nehemiah and his crew of builders. When the enemies started to menace them, Nehemiah reminded the people that their inspiration and protection came from the God who had given them this task. He wouldn't abandon the people who were obeying him.

God uses ordinary people to do extraordinary work for his kingdom even in the face of stiff opposition. If you focus on the size of your enemy, then God looks small. But if you focus on the power and greatness of God, your enemies look tiny. You can expect opposition whenever you are doing something for God.

Whether You Like It or Not

APRIL 15

Nehemiah 9:17— They refused to listen. They forgot the miracles you performed for them. . . . But you are a forgiving God, one who is compassionate, merciful, patient, and always ready to forgive. You never abandoned them.

*T*he children of Israel gave God no real reason to stick with them. They were ungrateful, immoral, idolatrous, and whiny. They didn't want God's help. But he never let them go. He never left them alone in the desert. He never completely rejected them. That is how it is with God. He loves us whether we like it or not because his compassion comes out of who *he* is, not who *we* are. It is comforting to be loved by a God whose love depends on his constancy, not our goodness.

A Moment with God

Come to God knowing he welcomes you. Thank him for his love, which is so much greater than human love.

For Further Reading: Nehemiah 9:5-37

Reason to Rejoice

*Nehemiah 12:43—
That day they . . .
rejoiced because
God had given them
reason to rejoice.
The women and
children rejoiced as
well. The sound of
rejoicing in
Jerusalem could be
heard from far
away.*

A Moment with God

Reflect on one good thing God has given to you or done for you lately. Take a moment to thank him.

*For Further Reading:
Nehemiah 12:27-47*

*H*as God given you reason to rejoice recently? Have you felt the benefits of his goodness? Maybe you completed a difficult project brilliantly or received a clean bill of health at your annual physical. Maybe it just hit you that your teenager really listens to you. Or maybe you got an unexpected bonus. God loves to give us good things. He delights in surprising us with unexpected joys. Like a parent wanting to give gifts to his or her beloved child, God's goodness overflows to us because of his love for us. It doesn't come with strings attached, and we don't have to earn it.

Who Has Influenced You?

*Esther 2:20—
Esther still had
not revealed her
family background
or nationality, as
Mordecai had
ordered her. Esther
always did
whatever
Mordecai told her,
as she did when
she was a child.*

God lovingly provided for Esther when her father and mother died by placing her in the care of her uncle Mordecai. This godly man tenderly cared for Esther, instructing her in God's ways and helping her learn how to act when she became part of the king's court. God's tender care extends to us in similar ways. He provides us with godly men and women who will show us how to love and serve him more deeply. Sometimes those godly mentors are our parents; sometimes they are friends who are more experienced than we are in hearing God's voice and in remaining faithful to him in new situations.

A Moment with God

Thank the Lord for the godly men and women he has placed in your life to nurture you and to help you remain faithful to him.

*For Further Reading:
Esther 2:1-23*

Timing

*Esther 4:14—
The fact is, even if
you remain silent
now, someone else
will help and
rescue the Jews,
but you and your
relatives will die.
And who knows,
you may have
gained your royal
position for a time
like this.*

A Moment with God

Ask God to help you grasp the opportunities for service which come your way this day.

*For Further Reading:
Esther 4:1–7:10*

One of the unique features of the book of Esther is its lack of direct references to God. The clearest allusion comes from Mordecai when he says that "someone else will help." Mordecai was certain that his niece, Esther, had the opportunity to play a role in God's plan. Why else would God have placed her on the throne?

How does God want to use us in his plans today? Perhaps there would be less confusion if we asked more often: What might be God's purpose in placing me where I am right now? Even more than our interest in personal accomplishments, we ought to be straining with eagerness to participate in what God wants to accomplish in such "a time like this."

A Part of the Majority

*Esther 9:1—
On the thirteenth
day of Adar, the
twelfth month, the
king's command
and decree were to
be carried out. On
that very day,
when the enemies
of the Jews
expected to
overpower them,
the exact opposite
happened.*

"Your opponent the devil is prowling around like a roaring lion" (1 Peter 5:8). "The world hates you" (John 15:19). "We are wrestling with . . . spiritual forces that control evil" (Ephesians 6:12). Scripture passages like these and others make it sound kind of scary to be a Christian, don't they? Yet one important fact should never be overlooked. Simply put, the size or strength of a believer's opponent makes absolutely no difference. Any Christian plus God equals a majority. Throughout history, God has demonstrated his protection of his people time and time again. When a situation is bleak and the odds are against us, God's protection is sure.

A Moment with God

Praise God for the fact that his protection is sufficient to defend you against any opposition.

*For Further Reading:
Esther 9:1-19*

109

The Game That Can- not Be Won

Job 2:3—
The LORD asked
Satan, "Have you
thought about my
servant Job? No
one in the world is
like him! He is a
man of integrity:
He is decent, he
fears God, and he
stays away from
evil. And he still
holds on to his
principles."

A Moment with God

Spend some quiet time with the God who knows all the secrets of your heart.

For Further Reading:
Job 1:1–2:6

*F*ollowing God isn't a game. It's not a roll of the dice. It's not an arm-wrestling match to determine strength. God can't be outsmarted or tricked. But Satan has never learned this lesson. Satan also doesn't comprehend how well God knows his children. Just as God knew Job, there is nothing the Father doesn't know about his children. Nothing about his children is hidden from God. Satan didn't understand that, either, and his lack of understanding defeated him. Even today, Satan hasn't learned this lesson. He continually tries to pull God's children away from their Father, just as he did with Job. Praise God that Satan will never succeed.

Children of the Father

APRIL 21

Job 5:17—
Blessed is the
person whom
God corrects.
That person
should not despise
discipline from
the Almighty.

Two-year-old children have a love/hate relationship with the word *"No!"* They love to say it but hate to hear it. They often cry as they struggle to live within the boundaries set by their parents. The short-lived struggle at two, however, is far better than a life without discipline. An undisciplined two-year-old could wander into the street, play with matches, or eat something poisonous. A loving parent disciplines the child out of love. Our Father God also disciplines us because he loves us. He sets the boundaries and disciplines us to stay within them. The struggle is often painful, but he is looking out for our best interests.

A Moment with God

Every time you experience God's discipline, you experience his love. Thank him for loving you enough to set boundaries.

For Further Reading:
Job 5:17-27

The One without Limits

APRIL 22

Job 21:22—
Can anyone teach
God knowledge?
Can anyone judge
the Most High?

Skeptics like to raise the question:
"Can God make a rock so big that
he can't lift it?" This question is
flawed because it begins, "can
God." If God exists, then God
can do anything. It is silly to
define what God can do by what
our limited minds can understand.

Job was right—no one can
fully understand God and how he
deals with people. Most questions raised questioning God's
power come from our desire to
believe only what we can explain
or control. God is beyond both
our explanation and control. He
is much bigger and more
complex than we can adequately
describe.

A Moment with God

Knowing God is an
ongoing discovery as
you study the Bible
and walk with Jesus
Christ each day.
Enjoy the journey!

For Further Reading:
Job 21:1-34

Unan-swerable

There are a lot of unanswerable questions in life: Why a young mother, in the prime of life, is suddenly stricken with cancer; why godly parents have a son who rejects all that is good and wholesome; why a businessman who has always put God first goes bankrupt. Though the answers we want may not be found in our lifetime, we do know *who* has the answers. Our God is the source of all wisdom and understanding. In his incredible wisdom, he has a good purpose for each of life's disasters. Knowing that he understands each tragedy completely means we can have peace, trusting him with the outcome.

Job 28:20–21,23— Where does wisdom come from? Where does understanding live? It is hidden from the eyes of every living being, hidden even from the birds in the air. . . . God understands the way to it. He knows where it lives.

A Moment with God

Praise God that no tragedy you face is outside the scope of his wisdom and understanding.

For Further Reading: Job 28:12-28

Do You Know?

APRIL 24

Job 37:16—
Do you know how
the clouds drift
(these are the
miracles of the one
who knows
everything)?

A Moment with God

Think about the link between the mystery that surrounds God and the wonder it generates. How does this affect your worship?

For Further Reading:
Job 37:14-24

Over two millennia later and we still cannot answer this question much better than Job himself. Sometimes it seems that the more we know, the more we don't know. One answered question yields another 20 questions yet to be answered. There is much about both creation and Creator that remains cloaked in mystery. God cannot be subjected to the scientific method and studied with all his qualities and traits catalogued. God is not a frog, pinned down on the waxed box of our personal laboratory. The means to understanding him is not dissection. It is in wonder and worship that we will come to know him best.

The Testimony of Nature

*Job 38:36—
Who put wisdom
in the heart or
gave understand-
ing to the mind?*

Job had lost almost everything.
What was God's response? He
took Job on a nature walk. *Look
around you, Job. Look at creation.
I am here. The evidence of me
and my control is everywhere in
nature. See the reasons you
should believe that you can trust
me. Look at the everyday examples of the fact that what I do, I
do well. Your life is in rags, but
the rags are in my hands, and I
will care for them as silk.* Walk
outside or look out a window and
see that God can be trusted with
the making of a world and the
guarding of your life.

A Moment with God

Look out a window
as you pray, and see
the imprint of a
deliberate creator.

*For Further Reading:
Job 38:31-38*

Bigger Than Life

Job 42:3—
"⌊You said,⌋ 'Who is
this that belittles
my advice without
having any
knowledge ⌊about
it⌋?' Yes, I have
stated things I
didn't understand,
things too
mysterious for
me to know."

A Moment with God

Rest in the fact that
the one who knows
the end from the
beginning is ruling
over you with love.

For Further Reading:
Job 42:1-6

*T*here comes a point in every
serious encounter with God that
we must concede our right to
have all the answers and accept
his right to be God. Like a child
who thinks $20 bills come from
automatic banking machines,
we're not able to see all that
goes on behind the scenes of
life. God's understanding alone
is complete. We can shake our
fists in the air, turn our backs to
him, take it out on our families,
or argue into the nighttime sky
till we're blue in the face. Surely
by now he's heard it all. But still,
he is Lord. He is God. And he
knows us better than we know
ourselves.

Husks

Psalm 1:6—
The LORD knows
the way of righteous
people, but the way
of wicked people
will end.

God knows. Nothing escapes his attention. God is fully aware. It is sheer arrogance or ignorance to live as if God overlooks what we do.

Wise people, this psalm states, live with God's word on their minds. They don't identify with those who live without fear of God. God "knows the way of righteous people" in the sense that he knows his own character. God preserves those who seek to be like him. God knows them and will allow them to know him eternally. Those who insist on settling for this life will last no longer than husks. The righteous will be planted; the wicked will be swept away.

A Moment with God

Lord, your knowledge of all my ways makes your kindness, mercy, and love all the more precious to me. Fill me with your righteousness.

For Further Reading:
Psalm 1:1-6

A Drop in the Bucket of Creation

Psalm 8:3-4—
When I look at
your heavens, the
creation of your
fingers, the moon
and the stars that
you have set in
place—what is a
mortal that you
remember him or
the Son of Man
that you take care
of him?

A Moment with God

Thank the Lord, the Creator of all things, that he grants significance on you by remembering you in the midst of his vast creation.

For Further Reading:
Psalm 8:1-9

*H*ave you ever tried to count the stars in the night sky? Have you ever wondered how many billions of galaxies exist beyond our own? Have you ever felt insignificant in the face of such a vast universe? Perhaps even more wondrous than the enormity of God's creation is that despite the enormity of creation, God remembers us and takes care of us.

The Gravity of the Situation

APRIL 29

Psalm 9:7—
Yet, the LORD is
enthroned forever.
He has set up his
throne for
judgment.

When a leaf separates from a branch, the leaf falls to the ground. A sheaf of papers tossed off a rooftop will float and scatter to the earth. Everything that goes up, as the saying goes, eventually comes down. It's gravity, and we are certain that it will not change. Just as we can be sure that gravity will pull us back to earth, we can be certain of God's righteousness. That certainty gives us confidence that God is a fair judge of hearts. Over and over, the Scriptures remind us of this truth. God knows what is right, because he is the originator of righteousness. How good it is to trust in a God who is fair!

A Moment with God

Express your gratitude to God for his righteousness. Let him know that you trust him to judge you in fairness.

For Further Reading:
Psalm 9:1-20

Our Refuge

*Psalm 16:1,8—
Protect me, O God,
because I take
refuge in you. . . . I
always keep the
LORD in front of
me. When he is by
my side, I cannot
be moved.*

A Moment with God

Are you hurting or afraid right now? Ask God to give you refuge. Praise him for being your protector.

*For Further Reading:
Psalm 16:1-11*

When you are in pain or trouble, do you despair or do you run to a trusted refuge? Those who trust in the Lord have the wonderful assurance that he is their protector. Like a fortress on a hill, a guide in the wilderness, or a lighthouse in a storm, he is there to mark your way and lead you safely through your trial. If you're discouraged or frightened, confused or lonely, don't lose hope! Fix your eyes on him. He will not let you be shaken off his chosen path, and his courage, peace, and confidence are yours for the asking.

Turning the Darkness to Light

Psalm 18:28—
O LORD, you light
my lamp. My God
turns my darkness
into light.

We need only read the daily newspaper or watch the evening news to realize how dark our world can be. Violence, war, poverty, hatred, and lawlessness seem to overwhelm us. Even in our personal lives we sometimes feel overcome by the darkness of discouragement. However, that's not the whole story. God has good news. He breaks into that darkness like a powerful beam of light and shows us the way out. His word of forgiveness and reconciliation brings hope to our personal lives and to the world.

A Moment with God

Reflect on ways God has turned your darkness into light. Thank him for his power.

For Further Reading:
Psalm 18:1-36

The Most Famous Song

Psalm 23:1—
The LORD is my
shepherd.
I am never in
need.

*T*hese famous words tell us volumes about our relationship with God. We are sheep—independent, headstrong, and often stupid. We have a limited understanding of our whole environment. God is the shepherd—our provider, defender, and guide. He gives us everything we need and stays right beside us through the most threatening experiences of life. If we are smart sheep, we learn to stay with the shepherd.

Why did God use the shepherd-sheep metaphor to describe his relationship with us? A shepherd knows the sheep, is close to the sheep, and loves the sheep. God wants us to know how close he wants to be to us.

A Moment with God

God has provided everything we need in this life. Remember who you are and thank God for who he is.

For Further Reading:
Psalm 23:1-6

Teaching a New Dog an Old Truth?

*I*t is God's truth that gives us guidance and sets our path. It is God's truth that heals us and helps us. It is God's truth that sets us free and binds us to him. We can talk of mercy and compassion, of emotions and feelings. But it is the unchanging truth of God and the integrity of his word that is our anchor. It's there for us to read, to delight in, to love, to play over in our minds, and to be changed by. Whether our lives are in shambles or in order, God's truth is the same.

MAY 3

Psalm 25:4-5—
Make your ways
known to me, O
LORD, and teach
me your paths.
Lead me in your
truth and teach
me because you
are God, my
savior. I wait all
day long for you.

A Moment with God

Use Psalm 25:4-5 as your prayer. Ask God to help you obey him.

For Further Reading:
Psalms 25:8-21

Dancing Lessons

Psalm 30:11—
You have changed
my sobbing into
dancing. You have
removed my
sackcloth and
clothed me with joy.

A Moment with God

Thank God that he does not abandon you in your troubles. He sees. He knows. He cares. And he comforts.

For Further Reading:
Psalm 30:1-12

The bomb blast that destroyed the federal building in Oklahoma City on April 19, 1995 claimed 168 lives. One of the survivors, who lost several family members in the explosion, was so injured in the rubble that doctors were forced to amputate a leg. What incredible grief she must have felt! But then one year later, she gave birth to a new baby. Her life was once again filled with joy. God chose to overshadow the former grief with new joy. He loves to do things like that. Are you overwhelmed with grief? Rest in his arms and know that he can turn your sobbing into dancing.

Surrounded!

Psalm 34:7—
The Messenger of
the LORD camps
around those who
fear him, and he
rescues them.

"You are surrounded!" If the words come from an enemy, they carry the threat of no escape. But what if we are encircled on every side by a powerful ally who places himself between us and the enemy? Now the phrase conveys safety. Like an efficient military force, God guards the perimeter of our lives.

But note the twist. The "fear" of those under God's protection is not toward the enemy but toward God. This respect comes from knowing that someone easily capable of destroying us and the enemy has chosen to rescue us.

A Moment with God

Ask the Lord for an awareness of his protection in your life today.

For Further Reading:
Psalm 34:1-22

Forever and Ever

Psalm 39:4-5—
Teach me, O Lord,
about the end of
my life. Teach me
about the number
of days I have left
so that I may know
how temporary my
life is. Indeed, you
have made the
length of my days
⌊only⌋ a few inches.

A Moment with God

Praise God for his eternal nature. Ask him to give you an eternal perspective on your everyday life.

For Further Reading:
Psalm 39:1-13

*A*s finite human beings, it is difficult—if not impossible—for us to fully understand God's eternal nature. When you think of longevity, who or what comes to mind? Perhaps it's George Burns, who lived to be 100. Or perhaps it's Methuselah, the oldest recorded human, who lived to be 969. Contrast that with God, who was around not only for Methuselah's 969 years but also for the foundation of the earth upon which Methuselah walked. Whereas humans are limited by time, God exists outside of time. He is eternal; he always has been and always will be.

"Do You Remember . . . ?"

*Psalm 44:1—
O God, we have
heard it with our
own ears. Our
ancestors have told
us about the
miracle you
performed in their
day, in days
long ago.*

*T*he best antidote to despairing in an impossible situation is to remember how God's power was made real in the past, both your past and the past of others. Remember how he fed millions of Jews in the middle of a desert. Remember how he healed your critically ill neighbor. Remember how he brought wholeness and growth to your divided church. Remember how he provided enough money to pay the rent when you were out of work. God's power to do the impossible is just as strong today as it was yesterday or even three thousand years ago. Since God never changes, you can have confidence and hope when you face today's impossible situations.

A Moment with God

Reflect on a time when God's power was made evident in your life. Thank him for the reminder of what he can and will do for you.

*For Further Reading:
Psalm 44:1-8*

Letting Go

*Psalm 46:10—
Let go ⌊of your
concerns⌋! Then
you will know that
I am God. I rule
the nations. I rule
the earth.*

A Moment with God

Giving up our
concerns to God
often serves to
convince us that he is
a God who cares for
us personally and is
"able, more than
able." Praise him for
his power in your life.

*For Further Reading:
Psalm 46:1-7*

D"Did you do this all by yourself?"
This is the most common question asked of a kindergarten child
presenting a piece of artwork to
the teacher. From our earliest
days we are encouraged to learn
to eat on our own, walk on our
own, use the bathroom on our
own, ride a bike on our own, with
the eventual goal of all goals . . . to
be on our own. It's no wonder that
we find it so hard sometimes to
let go of our own agendas and
watch God take care of it. Yet if
we don't develop this habit, we
are in danger of crediting our own
efforts or wisdom or planning for
something that happened only
through his great power.

Restorative Power

Psalm 51:10—Create a clean heart in me, O God, and renew a faithful spirit within me.

*D*oes your spirit seem dry? Is your heart bruised from unfaithfulness and failure? Are you burdened by guilt because of your sin? Perhaps that's what the psalmist was experiencing when he solicited God's healing. "Create a clean heart in me, O God." Can God actually take a broken heart and revive it, encourage it, make it new again? Of course, he can! He is, after all, the God of creation—the original creative genius. His power to create didn't end after the first six days. God's creativity is as limitless as the needs of his children. His restorative power is always on call.

A Moment with God

Are you thirsty for renewal? Ask God to renew your spirit.

For Further Reading: Psalm 51:1-19

All Eyes on You

*Psalm 56:8—
You have kept a
record of my
wanderings. Put my
tears in your bottle.
They are already in
your book.*

A Moment with God

Ask God to help you
always remember
that, even in your
darkest, loneliest
times, he is watching
over you.

*For Further Reading:
Psalm 56:1-13*

God, whom you might think has his hands full spinning solar systems and deposing dictators, always keeps his eye on you. He watches you when you lay awake at night and wonder why life is so hard, or as you long for the happiness you once knew. He notices your situation, writing each line in the book of his memory. Your ceiling may seem dark and silent, but God is watching . . . and waiting . . . and working. And one day, you'll wonder why you thought he wasn't.

Storm Warnings

*E*verybody has trouble, even Christians who have strong faith. But God is a stronghold where we can find help. He gives us assurance that he will never leave us or forsake us as we go through the difficulties. He reminds us that our relationship with him cannot be threatened by trouble. He gives us peace when we release our burdens to his care. He gives us courage and strength to continue down difficult paths. He also lifts us out of our depression and gives us joy knowing that our relationship with him is secure. For all these reasons we sing his praises and thank him for his steadfast love.

MAY 11

Psalm 59:16-17— But I will sing about your strength. . . . You have been my stronghold and a place of safety in times of trouble. O my strength, I will make music to praise you! God is my stronghold, my merciful God!

A Moment with God

What trouble are you facing right now? Praise God for his promise to be your stronghold and your place of safety.

For Further Reading: Psalm 59:1-17

131

The Safest Place

Psalm 62:8—
Trust him at all
times, you people.
Pour out your
hearts in his
presence. God is
our refuge.

A Moment with God

Tell God the things that steal your serenity, and let him be your sanctuary.

For Further Reading:
Psalm 62:1-12

God is the safest place you'll ever know. He is a warm, dry cave if you're lost in a storm. He is a warm embrace if you've been left alone. He is a smile in a sea of angry faces. He is a lit porch light in a dark neighborhood. God is the last safe turn before the dead end and the emergency landing strip before the engines fail. Whatever the threat, whoever the enemy, God is the safest place you can run to. He's the sanctuary for your need, whatever it is. You can run to him and be safe.

Getting a Clean Slate

*Psalm 65:3—
Various sins
overwhelm me.
You are the one
who forgives our
rebellious acts.*

*D*o you remember the shame and panic you felt when you were a young child and your parents found out you had done something wrong? You just ached for another chance to do it over again and this time to do it right. Sometimes life doesn't seem to have changed much from when we were children. The power of our sin still overwhelms us at times, and we wish we could start over and do it right. It's at that point of need that God touches our lives with his forgiving power. He takes our confessed sin and wipes it away, giving us a clean slate, a clean heart with which to have another chance.

A Moment with God

Knowing that God loves you and longs to forgive you, confess your sin to him and ask him to give you a clean heart.

For Further Reading: Psalm 65:1-13

The God Who Hears You

Psalm 66:20—
Thanks be to God,
who has not
rejected my prayer
or taken away his
mercy from me.

A Moment with God

Do you have a pressing need at this time? Go to God with it. Be sure to thank him for listening to you.

For Further Reading:
Psalm 66:16-20

*H*ave you ever asked for help and been rejected? Maybe you needed a loan, and the bank wouldn't even consider your request. Maybe you needed a listening ear, and your friend couldn't make time in her busy day. But there is one you can go to who will hear and answer you. God is faithful; he is always ready to make time for you. So be encouraged! He will not reject the prayers of those who pursue a right relationship with him. More amazing still, his answers to your prayers are full of his mercy—his answers will be better for you than anything you could imagine or hope for.

Solid As a Rock

*Psalm 71:3—
Be a rock on
which I may live, a
place where I may
always go. You
gave the order to
save me! Indeed,
you are my rock
and my fortress.*

After delivering the Sermon on the Mountain (Matthew 5–7), Jesus described two kinds of people: Those who listen and apply his words build their lives on a trustworthy foundation; those who listen but fail to apply Jesus' teaching build their lives on a sandy foundation.

In this psalm, what begins as a prayer, "Be a rock," becomes a declaration of faith, "you are my rock." No matter what the need, when we bring it before God, we come to realize he is the ultimate source. He will prove to be the one on which we may live. God's trustworthiness makes him the place where we may always go.

A Moment with God

Identify at least five times throughout the day when you can return to "the Rock" in prayer.

*For Further Reading:
Psalm 71:3-8*

Reward and Punishment

*Psalm 75:7—
God alone is the
judge. He punishes
one person and
rewards another.*

*P*eople who are unfamiliar with
God and the nature of Christianity
often ask, "How could a loving
God send good people to hell?"
However, when you appreciate
God's holiness, the question
becomes "How could a holy God
allow anyone into heaven?"
Because God is holy, he removes
himself completely from all sin.
He can have nothing to do with
unrighteousness. All sin demands
judgment and punishment. In his
love for us, God sent his Son to
face the judgment and take our
punishment. Those who believe
in Christ escape judgment; those
who don't believe face the wrath
of God's holiness.

A Moment with God

Praise God for the
fact that you are able
to talk and have
fellowship with him
whenever you
desire—all because
Christ faced the wrath
of God's holiness in
your place.

*For Further Reading:
Psalm 75:1-10*

The God Who Helps

*Psalm 77:11-12—
I will remember
the deeds of the
LORD. I will
remember your
ancient miracles. I
will reflect on all
your actions and
think about what
you have done.*

*I*s anything impossible for God? Is anything beyond his reach? Is any task too awesome for the miraculous God? The God who split the Red Sea like a piece of cloth . . . the God who created reverberating thunder . . . the God who dispensed manna for his children? For such a God as this, can our daily dilemmas be unconquerable? For such a God as this, can our puny problems be unsolvable? For such a God as this, can our little concerns outweigh his capacity to care and create solutions? Think about it.

A Moment with God

Tell God about the needs you have today. Wait on his reply.

*For Further Reading:
Psalm 77:1-20*

137

The Smile of God

MAY 18

*Psalm 80:3—
O God, restore us
and smile on us so
that we may be
saved.*

O(ften, when people attempt to imagine God, seated on his throne in all of heaven's splendor, they have a hard time picturing his face. To some, he is an angry God with a tight frown and piercing eyes of rage. For others, he is disinterested, caring little—if anything—about us. Many imagine him to be forever sad and brokenhearted over the things we have done. Very few picture God with a wide, toothy grin. Does God grin? Yes! When he decides to give us rest from our problems and strengthen us once again with his many blessings, he smiles on us. If you think that God spends most of his time being angry, then remember this: He smiles when he thinks of you.

A Moment with God

God's kindness comes in many forms. Reflect on how God has smiled on you, and thank him for each blessing.

*For Further Reading:
Psalm 80:1-19*

What Impresses God?

*Psalm 82:3-4—
Defend weak
people and
orphans. Protect
the rights of the
oppressed and the
poor. Rescue weak
and needy people.
Help them escape
the power of
wicked people.*

*H*ow do we impress God? Most of
our daily efforts to impress
others revolve around our
personal achievements—how
much we know, who we know, or
how much we own. Our quest to
attain significance in the eyes of
our peers leaves us unconnected
with God.

God values exactly the
opposite of what fuels the egos
of this world. God is concerned
with defending the weak,
protecting the oppressed, and
rescuing the needy. God loves
poor, helpless, needy underdogs.
To him these are the beautiful
and important people of this
world. God loves each person for
who they are, not for what they
have done.

A Moment with God

God loves you for
who you are—not
what you can
accomplish today.
Thank him for loving
the needy as much as
he loves those who
achieve success and
fame in this world.

*For Further Reading:
Psalm 82:1-8*

139

When Mercy's Tables Turn

Psalm 86:5—
You, O Lord, are
good and forgiving,
full of mercy toward
everyone who calls
out to you.

A Moment with God

Pray for God's mercy not only for yourself but for the people around you and the world you live in.

For Further Reading:
Psalm 86:1-17

When we are wronged by someone, we look to God for vengeance. When we wrong someone, we look to God for compassion.

When we have been betrayed, we look to God for protection. When we are the traitors, we look to God for forgiveness.

When we see hard-heartedness around us, we invoke God's judgment. When we find our own heart hard, we ask for God's tolerance.

When we see evil in the world, we cry for God's justice. When we see evil in our lives, we cry for God's mercy. And God's mercy is exactly what we receive.

Angels to Watch Over You

MAY 21

*Psalm 91:11-12—
He will put his
angels in charge of
you to protect you in
all your ways. They
will carry you in
their hands so that
you never hit your
foot against a rock.*

*D*id you know that you don't
have to be the president or an
organized crime boss to qualify
for bodyguards? God cherishes
you so much that he has given
his armies of angels the job of
protecting you. You may never
know the countless ways they
daily intervene on your behalf—
shielding you from accidents,
lessening the severity of a
tragedy, directing you to a safer
course. Since nothing can slip by
them or surprise them, you can
have confidence that when you
face pain or loss, it is part of
God's plan for you and never,
ever an accident.

A Moment with God

Reflect on the
amazing protection
God's angels give you.
Praise God for caring
for you in this way.

*For Further Reading:
Psalm 91:1-16*

God's Not a Theorem

Psalm 96:8—
Give to the Lord
the glory he
deserves.

W̲e often treat God like an academic subject. Sometimes we treat him like we treat Algebra. We open the book, study a bit, learn the rules, then go about the business of our day. This kind of treatment of God isn't right. He's not a lifeless theorem. He's not a good idea that someone has invented. He's not a cosmic set of laws. God is real and personal. He's beside you right now and is as real as the book you're holding.

Take a moment and look to your left and your right. God is there, beside you. He always is.

A Moment with God

Don't forget that God remains with you throughout the day. Thank him that he travels with you wherever you go.

For Further Reading:
Psalm 96:1-8

Caught Red-Handed

MAY 23

*Psalm 97:12—
Find joy in the
LORD, you
righteous people.
Give thanks to
him as you
remember how
holy he is.*

*I*f God hadn't made us righteous in his sight, the thought of his holiness would cause us to run from him. We'd avoid eye contact at all costs. Like being caught red-handed by a friend, we'd wish we could just disappear. But in truth God *has* caught us red-handed but has chosen to save us by his own red hands. By reaching out to us with the blood-stained hands of his Son, Jesus Christ, he caught us from plunging to our deaths. He has given his holiness to us, so that we would not be frightened away from him but be drawn closer to him.

A Moment with God

Take time to bask in the Lord's holiness today, thanking him for making it a place of warmth, not coldness.

*For Further Reading:
Psalm 97:1-12*

Belonging

*Psalm 100:3—
Realize that the
LORD alone is God.
He made us, and
we are his. We are
his people and the
sheep in his care.*

A Moment with God

In the words of
Psalm 23, do not call
God *Shepherd* until
you call him *Lord*.

*For Further Reading:
Psalm 100:1-6*

*I*f there is only one God, what
does that make us? People often
grudgingly admit to God's
existence without recognizing
what that implies about themselves. In fact, some claim to
believe in God while they behave
as if *they* were God!

This psalm of praise clarifies
some basic relationships. We are
to recognize that "the Lord alone
is God." He made us. He owns us.
He gives us personal worth as
people. And God cares for us. God
could treat us as property. Instead,
he gives us the marvelous privi–
lege of relating to our creator on a
personal, intimate level.

Forgive and Forget

MAY 25

*Psalm 103:8—
The LORD is
compassionate,
merciful, patient,
and always ready
to forgive.*

A careless driver cuts us off in traffic. A neighbor spreads damaging rumors about us. How do we deal with people who offend or cause problems for us? How well do we respond to apologies? Are we more likely to forgive and forget or to hold a grudge for a while? Most of us have probably nursed our share of grudges. So how remarkable is it that our holy God sits ever-ready to forgive any offense of which we repent? Knowing our sinful nature, God is still compassionate enough to forget forever all of our sins and disobedience against him—if we repent and ask him for forgiveness.

A Moment with God

Thank the Lord for the compassion he shows and his willingness to forgive sins. Consider how you might demonstrate similar compassion to those who sin against you.

*For Further Reading:
Psalm 103:1-22*

Our Praise-Worthy God

Psalm 105:2—
Sing to him. Make
music to praise
him. Meditate on
all the miracles he
has performed.

A Moment with God

Sing a song of praise
to the God of all
praise. Use your own
words or read aloud
Psalm 105.

For Further Reading:
Psalm 105:1-6

*R*emember the plaster handprint you made in kindergarten for your mom? Can you recall the joy you felt in offering it to her? Remember how you watched her face to catch her reaction? Offering praises to God brings him that same delight that you experienced as a youngster. God loves to receive the praises of his children. We are never nearer the Father than when we offer praises to him ... praises bring a smile to the face of heaven. Whether we're gifted in song or sing off-key, the praise God's children send heavenward is beautiful music to the Father's ears.

God Rescues Us

MAY 27

Psalm 107:6—
In their distress
they cried out to
the LORD. He
rescued them from
their troubles.

*A*s the Israelites wandered in the
desert facing enemies, danger,
and death, they cried out to God,
and he rescued them. The same
God who rescued the Israelites
stands ready to rescue us from
our distresses, whether that be a
struggling marriage, singleness,
infertility, chronic illness, financial
stress, or a rebellious child. God
has compassion for us when he
sees us in trouble. He wants us to
call out to him and to trust him to
rescue us. He always stands
ready to hear our cries for help.
We can count on him to rescue us.

A Moment with God

Think about the
distresses God has
rescued you from in
the past. Give him
your present trouble,
and trust him to
rescue you.

For Further Reading:
Psalm 107:1-32

The Rewards of Obedience

MAY 28

Psalm 112:1-2—Hallelujah! Blessed is the person who fears the LORD and is happy to obey his commands. His descendants will grow strong on the earth. The family of a decent person will be blessed.

A Moment with God

How has God blessed your obedience? Praise him for it!

For Further Reading: Psalm 112:1-10

God loves to bless us. However, many of his blessings have a prerequisite—obedience. According to his plan, it is in the very act of obedience that we fully experience the blessings that come from living rightly. When we obey his command to take care of our bodies, he may bless us with health and long life. If we obey his requirement to work hard and not be lazy, he may bless us by meeting our needs and giving us the satisfaction of a job well done. "Obedience has its own rewards" is in reality God's wonderful way of blessing those who seek to please him.

A Day in God's Life

*Psalm 113:5-8—
Who is like the
LORD our God?
He is seated on
his high throne. . . .
He lifts the poor
from the dust. He
lifts the needy from
a garbage heap.
He seats them with
influential people,
with the influen-
tial leaders of his
people.*

What's on God's schedule for today? A popular series of books uses remarkable photos to capture a typical day in the life of various cities and countries. What would a book on God show him doing during a 24-hour day? Psalm 113 paints a picture of God as the supreme ruler of the universe, who is also interested in each one of us. God intervenes in the lives of the poor and needy to assist them with their struggles. God rearranges society, mixing the poor with the rich and powerful. He is also busy bringing an inner joy to people who have lost the reasons to be happy. Looking beyond his own glory and majesty, God is active helping the people he created and loves.

A Moment with God

God cares! He sees the trials and struggles people are facing today. From his throne in heaven God extends his hand of help to those in need.

For Further Reading: Psalm 113:1-9

There Is None Stronger

*Psalm 118:14—
The LORD is my
strength and my
song. He is my
savior.*

*I*t is a waste if we spend our lives
cringing as if the bully of the
playground is after us, when our
big brother is the strongest guy in
school. God is a God of power and
might, of victory in battle. He
makes a way for his people to
hold their heads high and walk
with dignity. God's strength
sustains and precedes us. God's
strength protects and surrounds
us. God's strength shepherds and
guides us. God's strength saves
us from our enemies and ourselves. God's strength is a part of
every day that we live.

A Moment with God

Ask God to remind
you of his strength
throughout the day
when your strength
is not enough.

*For Further Reading:
Psalm 118:5-29*

I Still Believe

Psalm 119:41-42—
Let your blessings
reach me, O LORD.
Save me as you
promised. Then I
will have an answer
for the one who
insults me since I
trust your word.

*T*here is often a gap in time between a promise and its fulfillment. During this uncomfortable waiting period, clouds of doubt can dissolve trust in the one who made the promise. The psalmist faced this problem, calling on God to fulfill his promises when life became difficult. Others chided him for trusting in God. Had God forgotten? Did he care? Why didn't he fulfill his promises?

God is always faithful to fulfill his promises but he rarely does so by the human clock. He knows what is best, and he will faithfully keep his promises according to his perfect plan for your life.

A Moment with God

Thank God for his faithfulness in keeping his promises. Pray that he will help you wait on his timing.

For Further Reading:
Psalm 119:41-48

Powerful
Name

Psalm 124:8—
Our help is in the
name of the LORD,
the maker of
heaven and earth.

Names identify and describe.
They narrow the possibilities.
Titles and characteristics single
out a subject. There are many
kings but only one King of kings.
There are many "gods" but only
one "maker of heaven and earth."

David wrote this psalm to
help people prepare for worship.
He wanted them to remember
that help doesn't come by accident
or coincidence. Help comes from
the Lord. God's past help enlarges
his reputation, and as a result,
God has created quite a name for
himself. Where do you need help?
What troubles you? The maker of
everything invites you to look to
him when you need help.

A Moment with God

What help has come
to you recently which
deserves added
thanksgiving to the
Lord?

For Further Reading:
Psalm 124:1-8

Mount Yahweh

Psalm 125:1-2—Those who trust the LORD are like Mount Zion, which can never be shaken. It remains firm forever. ⌊As⌋ the mountains surround Jerusalem, so the LORD surrounds his people now and forever.

What places or situations are synonymous with safety and security in your life? Being hugged tightly by one of your parents? Lying in bed at night with the covers wrapped snugly around you? Sitting by a fireplace, warm and dry, on a cold, snowy night? Compare these forms of "security" with the protection of God, who surrounds his people like a mountain. Think about it: if the source of your safety is as impenetrable or unconquerable as the Himalayas or Rockies, what have you to fear?

A Moment with God

Think of some things that threaten your security or peace of mind. Thank God for the fact that his mountain of protection is capable of guarding you against all such threats.

For Further Reading: Psalm 125:1-5

Family Ties

*Psalm 133:1—
See how good and
pleasant it is when
brothers and
sisters live together
in harmony!*

A Moment with God

Is there someone you can settle a conflict with today? Ask God to show you how to be a peacemaker.

*For Further Reading:
Psalm 133:1-3*

Want to know what delights the heart of God? Care to learn the key to his smile? It's pretty simple, really. It's the breath of fresh air known as *unity*. When his children get along with one another and deeply care about each other, God is blessed. When disagreements are put aside, God is honored. When the people of God resolve conflicts, God is pleased. God is delighted when his children are more concerned with loving than fighting. What parent enjoys the bickering of his children? As our Father, God yearns to see his children embrace each other, their hearts unified.

Enduring Mercy

JUNE 4

Psalm 136:1-3—
Give thanks to the
LORD because he is
good, because his
mercy endures
forever. Give thanks
to the God of gods
because his mercy
endures forever.
Give thanks to the
Lord of lords
because his mercy
endures forever.

*T*he psalmist repeats himself over and over for good reason. God's mercy—his withholding the full punishment we deserve as sinners—is an awesome concept. That "his mercy endures forever" is incredible! There is no time limit or expiration date to it. It can't be used up or worn out. We can't do something so awful that it loses its effectiveness. It is there for us every time we fail, and it will be forever. Can you imagine our legal system pardoning a criminal more than once? What amazing love God must have for us that he offers us unlimited pardon.

A Moment with God

Reflect on the fact that God pardons you again and again. Thank him for his limitless mercy.

For Further Reading:
Psalm 136:1-26

A Father's Touch

JUNE 5

*Psalm 139:3—
You watch me
when I travel and
when I rest. You
are familiar with
all my ways.*

A Moment with God

There is nowhere
you can go that God
is not there with you.
Thank him for this
wonderful truth.

*For Further Reading:
Psalm 139:1-18*

*H*ave you ever tried to reason
with a fearful two-year-old? No
amount of reasoning or reassuring will do the trick. Turning on
the light in order to show that
there are no monsters hiding
under the bed will not always
meet the need. There is only one
thing that always works: the
presence of a parent. Try as you
might, there is no known substitute for a child simply being with
mom or dad.

Sometimes we are spiritual
two-year-olds and share similar
needs. We worry as we lie within
the confines of the bed. We're
scared about what lies out there
in the unknown. Only God's
constant presence and gentle
touch can quiet our soul and give
us rest.

Living Proof

*Psalm 142:3—
When I begin to
lose hope, you
₍already₎ know
what I am
experiencing.*

God in his infinite wisdom as the Creator of all things, already knew everything there was to know about the human experience from the time he made the world. But in order to make that truth more believable, he even came to earth as one of us and walked the choking sands of the Middle East. He engaged in the cultural debates of the day; he suffered the anger of his own people; he felt the distrust of his own family; he knew the betrayal of his friends; he experienced the agonizing death of a cross. He knows what it's like to hurt. And he's been there to prove it.

A Moment with God

No matter what you're going through, God has been there—and will go there—with you.

*For Further Reading:
Psalms 142 & 143*

Does God Play Fair?

*Psalm 145:17—
The LORD is fair in
all his ways and
faithful in every-
thing he does.*

Have you ever felt God has let you down? When friends betray you and life knocks you around, it's normal to question God's care. When life looks easy for others and hard for us, we can start to wonder if God plays fair.

God's promise to be fair and faithful to us doesn't mean we will all have the same amount of money, ability, or good health. It does guarantee that we have equal access and opportunity to what is truly important—knowing God and living with him forever. There is no discrimination or favoritism against those who seek him. The door is open for everyone. God's greatest demonstration of fairness is eternal salvation equally available to all peoples of the world—paid in full by the death and resurrection of his own Son, Jesus Christ.

A Moment with God

At the foot of the cross the ground is level. Thank God for his fairness. In our desperate need God is equally generous to us with his grace.

*For Further Reading:
Psalm 145:1-21*

Wisdom Is Speaking

God's wisdom speaks to us today. It asks us to follow because it knows if we do, we will be safe. God's wisdom is not a shackle. It is not a truth that, when we know it, keeps us from enjoying life. Rather, God's wisdom is what frees us to enjoy life fully. God's wisdom provides a framework in which laughter is full and freedom is for the taking. God's wisdom is what keeps us from disaster. God's wisdom is what shows us the way and keeps us safe until we arrive.

JUNE 8

Proverbs 1:33—But whoever listens to me will live without worry and will be free from the dread of disaster.

A Moment with God

Pray with an open mind, willing to obey God's wisdom.

For Further Reading: Proverbs 1:20-33

Looking for Wisdom

Proverbs 2:6—
The LORD gives
wisdom. From his
mouth come
knowledge and
understanding.

A Moment with God

Praise God for the breadth of his wisdom and for his willingness to share it.

For Further Reading:
Proverbs 2:1-22

We live in an information-driven society. We devour books, magazines, newspapers, television programming, and information on the Internet in an attempt to keep abreast of the latest news about any variety of subjects. But in our quest we sometimes settle for facts when we should be pressing on for wisdom—an ability to discern what to do with the facts. The true source of wisdom is God himself. He not only knows everything about the past and the future, but he understands what it all means. Rather than hoard that wisdom, God shares it with us. He invites us to share in his wisdom through his word and his will.

Trust and Obey

*Proverbs 3:5-6—
Trust the LORD
with all your
heart, and do not
rely on your own
understanding. In
all your ways
acknowledge him,
and he will make
your paths smooth.*

When it comes to trust, our choices are limited. We can trust God or we can trust something or someone who is not God. Our biggest temptation is to trust ourselves. We may even trust our limited understanding of God rather than place our trust in God himself. Part of trusting God with all our heart means knowing that God is greater in every way than we can understand.

So how then do we trust God? We acknowledge him in all our ways. We don't wait until our understanding falls short. We constantly seek God's participation in every part of life. As we do this, we won't always understand how, but we will discover to our delight that God will make our paths smooth.

A Moment with God

"Lord, help me not to just trust what I understand of you but to trust you far beyond my understanding."

*For Further Reading:
Proverbs 3:1-12*

Wise Advice

JUNE 11

Proverbs 4:5-6—Acquire wisdom. Acquire understanding. Do not forget. Do not turn away from the words that I have spoken. Do not abandon wisdom, and it will watch over you. Love wisdom, and it will protect you.

A Moment with God

Resolve to pursue wisdom. Ask God to strengthen your resolve.

For Further Reading: Proverbs 4:1-9

Have you ever been the recipient of excellent advice? Through the words of Solomon, God gives us some of the best advice there is: acquire wisdom, pursue it and hold on to it. Such a focus puts us in a position to learn the heart of God. He is the source of all wisdom, and he wants to share it with us. By giving us the Bible, the counsel of godly Christians, and a forum with him in prayer, he has made the path to wisdom plain to us. Don't miss out on the blessings of following his advice!

What's on Your Mind?

JUNE 12

Proverbs 5:21-22—Each person's ways are clearly seen by the LORD, and he surveys all his actions. A wicked person will be trapped by his own wrongs, and he will be caught in the ropes of his own sin.

*H*ow differently would you live your life if you knew that everyone you came in contact with—friends, family members, bosses, coworkers, and even total strangers—could read your mind? What if everyone you met always knew exactly what you were thinking, considering, and feeling? One of the theological terms used to describe God is *omniscient*, meaning he knows everything. *Everything* includes all of our thoughts and motivations. We may be able to fool or hide our true feelings from those closest to us, but not from God. Nothing we do is hidden from him.

A Moment with God

Praise God for the fact that he is all-knowing. Consider any adjustments that you might need to make in your thought-life.

For Further Reading: Proverbs 5:1-23

For Good or Evil?

Proverbs 6:16-19—There are six things that the LORD hates, even seven that are disgusting to him: arrogant eyes, a lying tongue, hands that kill . . . devising wicked plans, feet that are quick to do wrong, a dishonest witness . . .

A Moment with God

Spend a moment examining these cautionary words. How are you using your eyes, tongue, feet, hands, and mind to glorify God?

For Further Reading: Proverbs 6:16-19

*I*t's interesting that God has equipped his children with instruments for glorifying him. It's even more interesting to realize that these same instruments made for honoring the Father are capable of dishonoring God. The wise man of Proverbs enumerates the kinds of behavior that bring displeasure to the Lord of heaven as a reminder of what God expects from us. Either we can use our eyes, tongues, hands, minds, and feet to bring kindness and comfort to others, or we can use these instruments to lie, kill, devise wicked plans, and spread conflict. What will you do today?

The Helicopter-God

*Proverbs 7:1—
My son, pay
attention to my
words. Treasure
my commands that
are within you.*

You are stuck in traffic. You crane your neck to see if you can see the source of the problem, but every car is stopped for miles ahead. What do you do? Most likely, you turn on the radio to get an informed report from a traffic helicopter. They can see what you cannot and give you appropriate guidance. God's wisdom is like that. He can see things way up ahead of you that you cannot. He knows where the problems are. If you take the time to listen, he guides you along paths that keep you out of trouble. He alone knows the right path to take.

A Moment with God

God's wisdom is infinite. Praise him that he will always show you the way through your next jam.

*For Further Reading:
Proverbs 7:1-27*

God Rules— Period!

Proverbs 8:15-16—
Through me kings
reign, and rulers
decree fair laws.
Through me
princes rule, so
do nobles and all
fair judges.

A Moment with God

God reigns! Thank God that he is the supreme ruler of this world. All things are under his control.

For Further Reading:
Proverbs 8:1-31

*T*he governments of our world are a collection of democracies and dictatorships. These national leaders may not honor God or obey him, but their position of power is under his control. All rulers and leaders ultimately answer to the almighty, sovereign God. When rulers and leaders do seek God's wisdom, the people under their domain live together with justice and fairness in their society. God's will is done on earth. When leaders oppress their people and do evil, God is still in control and will ultimately bring them to judgment. Political and military power is worthless in the presence of Almighty God.

Where Does Wisdom Begin?

*T*o fear God is the beginning of wisdom. To know God is to have the understanding to use that wisdom. To fear God is to see a light that you want to follow. To know God is to follow that light. To fear God is to begin a journey. To know God is to both reach the destination and have the pleasure of the trip. To fear God is to buy a plane ticket. To know God is to soar. To fear God is the beginning of wisdom. To know God is to live wisely.

JUNE 16

Proverbs 9:10— The fear of the LORD is the beginning of wisdom. The knowledge of the Holy One is understanding.

A Moment with God

Ask God to teach you more about himself today.

For Further Reading: Proverbs 9:1-18

Twin Towers

JUNE 17

*Proverbs 10:29—
The way of the
LORD is a fortress
for an innocent
person but a ruin
to those who are
troublemakers.*

A Moment with God

Ask God to point you to someone who feels far from him today, and tell them how near he is.

*For Further Reading:
Proverbs 10:24-32*

*A*bright, sunny day is a blessing to someone wanting to go on a picnic but a curse to someone hoping to avoid mowing the grass. Just as there can be two different reactions to one sunny day, there can be two different reactions toward our one powerful God.

God is a tower of strength, a haven of rest for those who seek him as their only hope of rescue. But for those who insist on living by their own wits, God's fortress casts an irritating shadow. Their rejection becomes their ruin. Yet God is there, come rain or shine, always the same, with the same offer of protection. It just depends on how you look at him.

A Disgusting Stench

JUNE 18

Proverbs 11:1,20—Dishonest scales are disgusting to the LORD, but accurate weights are pleasing to him. . . . Devious people are disgusting to the LORD, but he is delighted with those whose ways are innocent.

What disgusts a holy and righteous God? The landlord who cheats his tenants. The politician who takes bribes. The marketing executive who sets up a smear campaign to undermine the competition. Dishonesty, deviousness, corruption—any form of unrighteousness—disgusts God. Such sin denies God's control as well as human worth, and he will not tolerate it. Just as we turn from a stench wafting from the sewer, he will turn away from those who practice such sin. But that isn't all. Just as we would be quick to remove a rotting animal carcass from our front step, so, too, is he quick to remove the source of unrighteousness. Those who practice such sin will not find God tolerant.

A Moment with God

Do the things that disgust God disgust you, too? Ask God to make you sensitive to unrighteousness.

For Further Reading: Proverbs 11:1-31

Honest to God

*Proverbs 12:2—
A good person
obtains favor from
the LORD, but the
LORD condemns
everyone who
schemes.*

A Moment with God

God is truth and
because of that he
can be trusted fully.
Ask him to show you
the areas in which
you are tempted to
scheme and then ask
for the faith needed to
trust in these areas.

*For Further Reading:
Proverbs 12:1-28*

Scheming is, at its core, a lack of trusting God. It is deceiving and tricking others. It's like laying a trap for someone, manipulating someone down a course of events toward a bad conclusion. In God's view lying and scheming are wrong. God does not want his children to have a lifestyle characterized by scheming because it implies a deep lack of trust. God is truth and wants truth to be the atmosphere in which we live and do our daily business. He wants a childlike honesty and sincerity to characterize our lives, leaving the results up to him.

R-e-s-p-e-c-t

Proverbs 13:14—
The teachings of a
wise person are a
fountain of life to
turn ⌞one⌟ away
from the grasp of
death.

The book of Proverbs serves us a banquet of common sense, practical wisdom, and valuable warnings. The unusual format of Proverbs doesn't lessen the fact that it is God's word. As such, our attitude toward the contents will create positive or negative results in our lives.

Like any great banquet, Proverbs must be more than a feast for the eyes. Until we fill ourselves with its spiritual meals by obedience, we will suffer the various hunger pangs of neglecting God's words.

A Moment with God

Lord, give me opportunities today to demonstrate my respect for your word by my obedience.

For Further Reading:
Proverbs 13:12-18

171

The Least of These

*Proverbs 14:31—
Whoever oppresses
the poor insults his
maker, but whoever
is kind to the needy
honors him.*

A Moment with God

Thank God for the fact that, even in his power and majesty, the Lord concerns himself with the poor and needy of this world.

*For Further Reading:
Proverbs 14:1-35*

*I*n our success-driven, celebrity-centered society, there is a tendency to assign deity status to stand-out performers in a given field. Successful pop musicians are labeled "rock gods"; talented athletes are called "sports gods." The irony is that when God chooses to align himself with human beings, often it's the poor, humble, and oppressed that he relates to. Nowhere in Scripture does the Lord say, "Blessed are the rich and powerful, for they shall have influence in this world." Instead, God concerns himself with the meek and down-and-out. Furthermore, God commands his people to follow his example of showing mercy on the poor and needy.

In the Warmth of the Son

JUNE 22

Proverbs 15:29— The LORD is far from wicked people, but he hears the prayers of righteous people.

*T*he holiness of God is like the sun: its brilliance constant, its power undeniable, its light unchangeable. Though clouds may obscure it temporarily, the sun is unblemished. Likewise, Satan may attempt to eclipse the holiness of God, but God is not hidden from his children. But the similarities end when we consider our distance from the sun and from God. For though the sun seems close, we could never reach its fiery shores. God, on the other hand, is as near as a whispered prayer. His holiness keeps him at arm's length from evil, but the prayers of righteous people bring him close.

A Moment with God

Today, thank God for listening to your prayers. Ask him to guide you toward righteous living.

For Further Reading: Proverbs 15:3,8-9,28-31

Who Is Really in Charge?

Proverbs 16:9—
A person may plan
his own journey,
but the LORD
directs his steps.

A Moment with God

Offer your plans and schedules to God, trusting him to lead you into experiences that have eternal value.

For Further Reading:
Proverbs 16:1-16

Most of us work hard at being in control. Armed with daily planners and goals, we move into each day with resolve and focus. When our schedules get disrupted, or when our to-do lists get hijacked by unexpected needs and demands, we get crabby and frustrated. Sounds hectic, doesn't it? How much better to realize that, while planning can be a helpful tool, God ultimately controls our lives. He knows not only who we are but also how we should be spending our time and energy. When we yield control of our lives to God, he brings meaning and purpose to our activity and to our relationships.

Purified
by Fire

*Proverbs 17:3—
The crucible is for
refining silver and
the smelter for
gold, but the one
who purifies
hearts ⌊by fire⌋is
the LORD.*

N obody likes hard times. When
life gets rough, we shouldn't jump
to the conclusion that God has
abandoned us. God sees beyond
all of our imperfections and
recognizes the "gold" and "silver"
in us. He brings out our best
when we feel life's pressure, and
as a result, we learn to rely on
him. The trials God allows in our
lives refine our strength and
character.

God loves us enough to want
the best for us even when it
means it might be painful for us.
He is a good coach, pushing his
players through demanding
practice sessions to build the
endurance and skill necessary to
compete in the game.

A Moment with God

Thank God for using
hardships and
difficulties to build his
character into you.

*For Further Reading:
Proverbs 17:1-6*

A Sure Refuge

*Proverbs 18:10-11—
The name of the
Lord is a strong
tower. A righteous
person runs to it
and is safe. A rich
person's wealth is
his strong city and
is like a high wall
in his imagination.*

A Moment with God

What do you find
yourself depending
on? Focus on your
true refuge—God.
Thank him for being
there for you.

*For Further Reading:
Proverbs 18:9-24*

Solomon reminds us that God is
the one we can count on when we
need refuge. Yet how many of us
find ourselves depending on the
imaginary protection of temporary things—our looks, our jobs,
our savings—forgetting that good
looks disappear, good workers
get laid off, and money gets used
up. These fragile refuges will fail
us, leaving us vulnerable when
we need help the most. Our God,
however, is a refuge that is real
and will never fail us. He is
always there for us. He won't
disappear; he can't be laid off,
and the security he offers can't
be used up.

The Unchanging God

*Proverbs 19:21—
Many plans are in
the human heart,
but the advice of the
LORD will endure.*

*H*umans are busy about their own plans. One day they follow one plan. Another day they follow a different plan. This differs from God. God stays the same: his principles do not change. He doesn't follow moods that swing like a pendulum. He doesn't refocus with each new piece of information. God is complete. His counsel is consistent. His wisdom is like a rock that stays steady in a storm. His course and his intent are set, and he doesn't waver. He is resolute in his good will, unstoppable in his salvation.

A Moment with God

Ask God what you should do about the parts of your life that puzzle you. Trust him for answers.

*For Further Reading:
Proverbs 19:17-22*

Godly Disgust

Proverbs 20:10—
A double standard
of weights and
measures—both
are disgusting to
the LORD.

A pet peeve is something that
really gets on our nerves—like a
driver who cuts us off, or a check-
out line that takes forever, or an
in-law who won't go away. Some
pet peeves run deeper, into
downright disgust—like child
molesting, or war-torn countries
where babies die, or a drunk
driving accident that claims lives.
God, too, has a list of pet peeves.
One is dishonesty; it disgusts
him. Sin itself revolts God. He
never hates the sinner, but he
always hates the sin. He knows
the damage it can do to us, so he
despises it completely.

A Moment with God

God can help you
overcome any sinful
habit. Praise him for
his disgust for sin
and his love for you.

For Further Reading:
Proverbs 20:1-30

Authority

M
Most of us work for someone.
Sometimes we feel like we're at
the bottom of a pile. We may be
tempted to conclude that our lives
are at the whim of those in
charge. The question we need to
ask is, "Who's really in charge?"

Elsewhere, God's word
instructs us to pray for those over
us (1 Peter 2:13-25). Why? Prayer
gains us access into the true
Supreme Court. We can appeal to
ultimate authority. We can bring
both our complaints and our
concerns for our bosses into
God's presence.

As we pray for those over us,
God may show us a lot about why
he has placed us where he
chooses. We will also be able to
see who is really in control.

Proverbs 21:1—
The king's heart is
like streams of
water. Both are
under the LORD's
control. He turns
them in any
direction he
chooses.

A Moment
with God

Pray by name for
those to whom you
are most directly
responsible today.

For Further Reading:
Proverbs 21:1-3

Good Guys and Bad Guys

*Proverbs 22:12—
The LORD's eyes
watch over
knowledge, but he
overturns the
words of a
treacherous person.*

*I*n the movies and on TV, it's
usually a safe bet that in the end
the good guys will win and the
bad guys will get what's coming to
them. Unfortunately, that's not
always true in real life.

God assures us, however,
that the situation is temporary.
Not only does he see everything
that goes on, he promises to
reward righteousness and punish
unrighteousness. Even though
evildoers may seem to prosper
now, they will face God's justice in
the end.

A Moment with God

Praise God for the
fact that he rewards
and punishes
everybody according
to his or her acts.

*For Further Reading:
Proverbs 22:1-29*

Truth: a First Step

O Over and over again, Scripture reminds us that truthfulness and honesty are the basic ingredients of righteousness. A person who cannot be truthful cannot be trusted. And in order for God to trust his children, he must hear only truth from their lips. God is a lover of truth because it is impossible for him to lie. In his righteousness he models for us the essence of truthfulness. Truth, then, must be a fundamental goal of the God-seeker or the God-follower: truth helps us know and understand God.

JUNE 30

Proverbs 23:16—My heart rejoices when you speak what is right.

A Moment with God

Have you thanked God today for his truthfulness? Praise him today for being a God of truth.

For Further Reading: Proverbs 23:12-25

The Grace to Continue On

*Proverbs 24:16—
A righteous person
may fall seven
times, but he gets
up again.*

**A Moment
with God**

Ask God to help you
never lose your fear
of falling—nor your
courage to get up
again.

*For Further Reading:
Proverbs 24:1-22*

Good is not surprised by human
sin. He, our maker, knows more
than anyone else how weak and
willing we can be in the face of
life's temptations. He makes his
overcoming power available to
any believer who will abandon
self-reliance and become a willing
servant, one who doesn't simply
apply God's strength but surren-
ders to it. It is a transformation,
though, that must often be
performed amid the fires of
failure and defeat—failures that
would be fatal, crashes that would
cripple us—were it not for God's
unfailing forgiveness.

The Only Just Judge

Proverbs 25:21-22—
If your enemy is
hungry, give him
some food to eat,
and if he is thirsty,
give him some
water to drink. ₍In
this way₎ you will
make him feel guilty
and ashamed, and
the LORD will
reward you.

*E*ver want to get revenge? Ever want to pay back someone for hurting you? In these situations God wants us to leave the judging of wrongs and the exacting of payment and punishment to him. He is a just God; he never convicts someone wrongly, and his punishment always fits the crime. Instead of taking matters into our own hands when we've been wronged, God asks us to do good to the one who has wronged us. By doing so, we avoid the sins of anger and retaliation, our kind actions make an offender face his guilt, and we receive a blessing from God. God's judicial system sounds like a profitable one, doesn't it? Leave justice in the hands of the only just judge.

A Moment with God

Think of a time when you retaliated for a wrong done to you. Ask God to help you to take kindness as your motto the next time and leave judgment in his hands.

For Further Reading:
Proverbs 25:8-10,
21-22

What You See Is What You Get

JULY 3

Proverbs 26:23—
ₗLikeₗ a clay pot
covered with cheap
silver, ₗsoₗ is
smooth talk that
covers up an evil
heart.

A Moment with God

Thank God that he is completely what he says he is. As his child, ask him for the same integrity in your own life.

For Further Reading:
Proverbs 26:20-28

God is the genuine article. There is a perfect match between what he does, what he says, and what he is. There is no need to wonder whether, when we get him home, a lesser version will somehow appear. There is full integrity with God. Kick the tires all we want, we will only be pleasantly surprised by what we find. And because this integrity is characteristic of God, he wants it also to be characteristic of his children. He doesn't want us to be full of pretense. But he doesn't ask us to strip off the silver from our pot of clay, he asks us to allow him to change that clay to solid gold.

No Pain, No Gain

Proverbs 27:17—
⌐As⌐iron sharpens
iron, so one
person sharpens
the wits of another.

N"No Pain, No Gain" reads the sign in the gym. We cannot get stronger by taking the soft road. When life gets tough, we are tempted to blame God: "If he really cared about me, how could he let me struggle through such trials and troubles?" God uses other people in our lives to make us stronger, sharper, and more effective. God wants to bring out the best in us. In the trial, he is faithful not to let any problem even touch us beyond what we are ready to handle. Surprisingly, good can come out of life's difficulties when God is our guide.

A Moment with God

C. S. Lewis said, "God whispers to us in our pleasure and shouts to us in our pain." Thank God for using your problems to help you grow stronger.

For Further Reading:
Proverbs 27:1-27

Rules, Rules, Rules!

*Proverbs 28:4—
Those who
abandon ⌊God's⌋
teachings praise
wicked people, but
those who follow
⌊God's⌋ teachings
oppose wicked people.*

A Moment with God

Ask God to show you the times today when you need to apply his instruction.

*For Further Reading:
Proverbs 28:4-28*

God's teaching is not a theory, a whim, a suggestion, a hypothesis. God's instruction is not a random rule book meant to impose control with no regard for the lives of his people. God gives instruction about what kind of people he wants his children to be, what kind of lives he wants them to live, what kind of legacies he wants them to leave. God gives the instruction because he loves his children and, while he knows they won't always follow, he wants to give them the best start possible.

An Audience with the Supreme Judge

*Proverbs 29:26—
Many seek an
audience with a
ruler, but justice for
humanity comes
from the LORD.*

When children are mistreated, when the poor are exploited, when evil goes unpunished, when powerful people take advantage of those who are weak, we feel a need to right the wrong. And when our human systems of justice fail to balance the scales, we get frustrated. Proverbs suggests that instead of looking to our rulers to mete out justice, we should ultimately look to the Lord. He is the ultimate judge; he is the supreme court of law. We can trust the Lord to use both his mercy and his power to bring justice to situations beyond our control.

A Moment with God

Reflect on situations that you feel need to be rectified. Give those situations to God, trusting him to be a just judge.

*For Further Reading:
Proverbs 29:1-27*

Weariness

*Proverbs 30:1—
The words of Agur,
son of Jakeh. Agur's
prophetic revela-
tion. This man's
declaration:
"I'm weary,
O God. I'm weary
and worn out,
O God."*

A Moment
with God

When I am weary,
Lord, and at my
lowest ebb, remind
me to turn to you.

*For Further Reading:
Proverbs 30:1-6*

Agur's only chapter in the Bible
begins with an honest sigh—"I'm
weary, O God." He repeats the
thought. Then he gives details!
Does God want to hear this?

Too often we use weariness
as a reason for *not* praying. In
fact, the prayer of weariness may
be one of the least-used avenues
of conversation with God. But
weariness is often good because
it reminds us that we need to
depend on God. But if we never
approach God on this basis, we
are overlooking our true condition and missing God's real
comfort. Some of the best times
for prayer come when we feel
least like praying.

The Ultimate Counsel

Proverbs 31:8-9—
Speak out for the
one who cannot
speak, for the
rights of those who
are doomed. Speak
out, judge fairly,
and defend the
rights of oppressed
and needy people.

One of the most familiar elements of any crime drama is the reading of the Miranda Rights: "You have the right to remain silent. . . ." A later provision of the Miranda Rights is as follows: "If you cannot afford an attorney, one will be provided for you." One of the hallmarks of the American judicial system is guaranteed representation for all. If a person is too poor to afford an attorney, a public defender is assigned to the case. In the same way, God protects the rights of all of his people—especially the poor and needy. If you are needy, take comfort in the fact that God is concerned about your rights. If you're not needy, allow yourself to be used by God on behalf of others who are less fortunate than you are.

A Moment with God

Thank the Lord for his special concern for the rights of the needy and oppressed.

For Further Reading:
Proverbs 31:2-9

Simple Pleasures

Ecclesiastes 2:24-25—
There is nothing
better for people to
do than to eat,
drink, and find
satisfaction in their
work. I saw that
even this comes
from the hand of
God. Who can eat
or enjoy themselves
without God?

A Moment with God

What simple
pleasure have you
been too busy to
enjoy? Ask God to
give you his
perspective on what
is important.

For Further Reading:
Ecclesiastes 2:4-26

*D*o we ever take time to really
enjoy the simple pleasures of
life— a gorgeous sunset, children
laughing, a summer picnic with
our families. Far from being
meaningless or trite, these
pleasures have intrinsic value
because God values them. As
Solomon comes to recognize,
everything in life is meaningless
without God, but with God even
the simplest, most basic of life's
events have splendor and value.
It's easy to dismiss simple joys as
a waste of our time as we strive to
accomplish "meaningful" things.
But remember, God created such
joys for us to enjoy. Making the
most of them puts us in touch
with their Creator and gives us a
glimpse of his perspective on
what is important in life.

Turn, Turn, Turn

*Ecclesiastes 3:1—
Everything has its
own time, and
there is a specific
time for every
activity under
heaven.*

*A*dear friend receives a grim
diagnosis. You pray for healing,
yet improvement does not come.
A relationship is strained, and you
wonder why reconciliation does
not float down from heaven. You
long for a promotion at work, but
your supervisors seem unaware
of your accomplishments.

Has God gone on sabbatical?
Is he perhaps in need of a battery
change so that he can work faster,
better, harder? No, the answer is
that his timing is not always our
timing. Knowing the complete
picture and what is best for all
persons concerned, God works in
a way that is best for each person.
Do not fight his schedule; trust
his sense of timing.

A Moment with God

Ask God to help you
wait patiently as you
learn more about
his timing.

*For Further Reading:
Ecclesiastes 3:1-8*

Ecclesiastes 7:14—When times are good, be happy. But when times are bad, consider this: God has made the one time as well as the other so that mortals cannot predict their future.

A Moment with God

Thank God that, even though you are not in control of your circumstances, he is. Trust in his wisdom.

For Further Reading: Ecclesiastes 7:11-29

The Good, the Bad, and the Ugly

*H*uman nature tells us to be thankful when we are happy and to find someone to blame when we are not. God often is the one who gets the blame for our unhappiness. After all, he is in control of everything, so why do bad things happen?

It is not God's fault—it is his wisdom. God knows what he is doing, even if we do not. He is teaching us to trust in him and not our circumstances. A relationship with God is like a marriage—we follow him for better or for worse. Tough times help us remember to depend on God and not ourselves.

One Appointment You Won't Miss

*T*he biggest evaluation of our lives will happen when we stand before God to give an account for our lives. It will be the most sobering moment of our existence.

God's judgment is just and fitting because, as Creator, he gave us our life. The promise of judgment reminds us that God considers our time here on earth an important investment. He cares enough to evaluate how we used what he gave to us.

On our own, we wouldn't receive a good evaluation. Sure, we've done some good things, but our many sins would be enough to keep us from receiving God's favor. Thankfully, God has planned for that moment by sending Jesus to pay for sins and guarentee God's children a heavenly reward.

Ecclesiastes 11:9b— Follow wherever your heart leads you and whatever your eyes see. But realize that God will make you give an account for all these things when he judges everyone.

A Moment with God

What you do with your life really matters to God. Thank God for giving you the opportunity to live and for providing his own son to stand with you on the day of judgment.

For Further Reading: Ecclesiastes 12:1-14

Passion and Desire

*Song of Songs 8:6—
Wear me as a
signet ring on your
heart, as a ring on
your hand. Love is
as overpowering
as death. Devotion
is as unyielding as
the grave.*

A Moment with God

Take time to thank
God for passionately
loving you.

*For Further Reading:
Song of Songs 8:4-7*

*T*he fact that God created us in his image teaches us something about him. He gave us the capacity for passion, for love more overpowering than death, and for devotion as unyielding as the grave. And so we know that the same God who made us with this passion, knows this passion himself. He also loves with determination. He devotes himself with unyielding devotion. He loves the way he wants to be loved— stubbornly and unyieldingly.

You're Being Used

*Isaiah 6:8—
Then I heard the
voice of the Lord,
saying, "Whom
will I send? Who
will go for us?" I
said, "Here I am.
Send me!"*

*E*specially if you're a perfection-
ist—which God definitely is—it's
painful to turn a job over to
someone else, knowing that they
probably won't do it just the way
you would have done it. Yet God,
who is above us, chooses daily to
delegate his work to people like
us. Why? Because if anyone were
to see God, he or she would die.
But when people see him in us—
when the love, truth, or compassion of the Lord comes wrapped
in next-door-neighbor flesh and
blood—they can see it and accept
it. They can believe and live.

A Moment with God

God wants to use
you in fulfilling his
plan. Ask him to start
preparing you today
for your next job.

*For Further Reading:
Isaiah 6:1-13*

A Royal Birth

JULY 15

*Isaiah 9:6—
A child will be
born for us. A son
will be given to us.
The government
will rest on his
shoulders. He will
be named:
Wonderful
Counselor, Mighty
God, Everlasting
Father, Prince of
Peace.*

A Moment with God

Address God through prayer by each of these four titles: Wonderful Counselor, Mighty God, Everlasting Father, Prince of Peace.

For Further Reading: Isaiah 9:2-7

What better time to celebrate Christmas than July? The incarnation of God transcends all seasons! His titles stretch our understanding. His glory awakens awe, yet he became one of us— born for us, given to us.

Jesus is the Word of God (John 1:1) and the truly wonderful counselor. He demonstrated his might as God when he created our world (Colossians 1:16). His eternal care for us defines the very meaning of Father (John 17:1-26). Jesus promised us incomparable peace (John 14:27). He is truly worthy of worship.

Count Your Blessings

Isaiah 14:1—
The LORD will have
compassion for
Jacob and again
choose Israel. He
will resettle them in
their own country.
Foreigners will join
them and unite
with the descen-
dants of Jacob.

*D*oes it ever seem that God blesses some people more than others? God's chosen people, the Israelites, were the recipients of countless blessings, even when they didn't deserve them. However, it was God's plan to bless the whole world through the Israelites. Through conquest, exile, and invasion, the Israelites introduced the nations of the world to God: an incredible blessing. And it was through an Israelite family that the Messiah came to save the world—the greatest blessing of all. God blesses those who make him Lord in their lives. But remember, the greatest blessing of all is one we all have equal access to—Jesus Christ.

A Moment with God
Ask God to use you to bless someone else.

For Further Reading:
Isaiah 14:1-23

197

Bump in the Night

Isaiah 21:11b-12—
Someone is calling
to me . . . "Watch-
man, how much of
the night is left?"
The watchman
answers, "Morning
is coming, and
night will come
again. If you need
to ask, come back
and ask."

A Moment with God

God's light is more powerful than any darkness this world can produce. Ask him to bring his light to bear on what stands in the shadows of your life.

For Further Reading:
Isaiah 21: 6-12

Can you remember being a child and lying in your bed at night afraid? You wondered in the dark how much longer that darkness would linger?

We are still children, but the darkness in which we sometimes find ourselves does not always correspond to the hands of a clock. If we will simply call out of our personal night, we will hear the same words of the watchman: As surely as morning follows the darkest night, Jesus the Morningstar will bring in the morning light.

No More Tears

Isaiah 25:8—
He will swallow up
death forever. The
Almighty LORD will
wipe away tears
from every face,
and he will remove
the disgrace of his
people from the
whole earth. The
LORD has spoken.

Humanity's two greatest enemies were sin and death. When Christ came to earth, he lived a sinless life; he then gave his life as a sacrifice to pay the price for our sin. In doing this, Christ defeated the power of sin. Three days after his crucifixion, Christ rose from the grave. In doing this, he defeated the power of death.

Because of God's unlimited power, those who believe in his Son can ultimately have hope in the face of death. The temporary tears of mourning are wiped away by the realization that all believers will live eternally in the presence of God. Death is not final. Sin won't always cling to us. When we leave this earth and enter heaven, we'll be entering a perfect place— a new home without sin or death!

A Moment with God

Praise the Lord for his power over death and the ultimate hope he offers for eternal life.

For Further Reading:
Isaiah 25:1-12

Rising to the Occasion

*Isaiah 30:18—
The LORD is waiting
to be kind to you.
He rises to have
compassion on you.
The LORD is a God
of justice. Blessed
are all those who
wait for him.*

A Moment with God

When has God blessed you with his compassion? How did you experience his strength and kindness?

*For Further Reading:
Isaiah 30:15-18*

A toddler climbs up on the kitchen counter, looking for cookies. On the other side of the room, Mom is putting the finishing touches on dinner. Meanwhile, toddler continues his quest. His unsteady little body begins to teeter on the edge of the counter. With her maternal antennae, Mom senses danger. The child begins to fall, and Mom springs into action, catapulting herself over anything else in her path. At that moment, her primal motivation is to prevent her toddler's pain. And that's what this passage reminds us: God wants nothing more than to rescue and comfort his children. He "rises" to the occasion—just as we would expect any loving parent to do.

Something to Count On

Isaiah 33:2—
O LORD, have pity
on us. We wait
with hope for you.
Be our strength in
the morning. Yes,
be our savior in
times of trouble.

*L*ife can sometimes feel over-whelming as we suffer through painful relationship breakdown, financial difficulty, debilitating illness, or family conflict. In the middle of the uncertainties, we can confidently pray this prayer: O Lord, be our strength in the morning, be our savior in the times of trouble. We can count on God to give us strength to face each day's challenges. We may not find the breakthrough to that broken relationship today or the solution to that financial stress, but we can go into the day with the confidence that God will walk with us through whatever we will face.

A Moment with God

Take God's hand and thank him for walking with you through whatever troubles you face today.

For Further Reading:
Isaiah 33:2-10

The Whole World's in His Hands

*Isaiah 37:20—
Now, LORD our
God, rescue us
from Assyria's
control so that all
the kingdoms on
earth will know
that you alone are
the LORD.*

*T*he children are right when they sing, "He's got the whole world in his hands." Every ruler and nation are under God's control. Even those national leaders who ignore or oppose God are subject to his almighty power. God hears the prayers of his people from all corners of the earth and responds to their pleas for peace and freedom. Just as he intervened in the history of Israel, God answered the prayers of his people when the Communist control of Eastern Europe and Russia collapsed. Where God's name was once outlawed now people worship him openly in freedom.

God intervenes in the course of history. In his perfect time God breaks down the walls that oppress his people.

A Moment with God

Where do you see God working among the nations and leaders of this world? Praise God for his sovereignty over all nations and for his intervention on behalf of his people.

*For Further Reading:
Isaiah 37:1-38*

202

"I Am with You"

Over and over again in the Bible, God says, "I will be there for you." He promises his presence, and that is what he gives. In this way he lets us know over and over again that he is not about fixing circumstances but rather building relationships. God's greatest act of love, after giving his Son, is his presence with us. And his presence is a promise we can count on whether we sense it or not, whether we think about it or not, whether we feel it or not. "Don't be afraid, because I am with you."

JULY 22

Isaiah 41:10—Don't be afraid, because I am with you. Don't be intimidated; I am your God. I will strengthen you. I will help you. I will support you with my victorious right hand.

A Moment with God

Any time you feel alone today, thank God for his presence.

For Further Reading: Isaiah 41:9-14

Greater Than a Mother's Love

JULY 23

*Isaiah 49:15—
Can a woman
forget her nursing
child? Will she
have no compas-
sion on the child
from her womb?
Although mothers
may forget, I will
not forget you.*

A Moment with God

Reflect on the truth
that God will never
abandon his
children. Thank him
for his faithfulness.

*For Further Reading:
Isaiah 49:14-26*

We've all heard at least one story
about a mother giving her life to
save her child. The incredible
bond between mother and child
is legendary. It would seem
impossible that any normal
mother could ever harm or
abandon her child. Yet God says
it is more likely for a mother to
forget her own child than it is for
God to forget his children. What
a picture of faithfulness! What
incredible love! When you are
tempted to think God has
washed his hands of you because of something you've done
or said, remember this: If you
are his child, there is *nothing*
that will make him leave you.

True Empathy

*Isaiah 53:3—
He was despised
and rejected by
people. He was a
man of sorrows,
familiar with
suffering. He was
despised like one
from whom people
turn their faces,
and we didn't
consider him to be
worth anything.*

The doctor's diagnosis is horrifying, and the prognosis is grim. An unexpected fire claims everything you own. The phone rings in the middle of the night with heart-stopping news. Problems like these cause great suffering. Does God understand? Yes. He knows exactly how you feel. When Jesus walked on this earth, he faced countless trials. He understands the deepest sorrow and the greatest suffering because he experienced a human life and death. And he knows the way out because he has been through this before.

A Moment with God

God is intimately acquainted with your suffering. Pray that he will show you how to make it through it all.

For Further Reading: Isaiah 53:1-12

Attention

*Isaiah 59:1—
The LORD is not
too weak to save
or his ear too
deaf to hear.*

A Moment with God

Confession frequently clears the lines of communication with God.

*For Further Reading:
Isaiah 59:1-11*

*T*hose who don't know God seldom understand prayer. They may tolerate prayer as a form of self-delusion, but they doubt prayer has any effect because they can't imagine a God who listens and acts. Christians don't pray because they believe they can control God. They pray because God has commanded them to do so (1 Thessalonians 5:17). And God never fails to hear their prayers.

We may doubt, but we don't have to. We may get impatient, but that doesn't help. Rather, once we have prayed, we need to trust God to answer.

Ready and Waiting

*Isaiah 65:1-2—
I was ready to
answer those who
didn't ask. I was
found by those who
weren't looking for
me. I said, "Here I
am! Here I am!"
to a nation that
didn't worship me.
I stretched out my
hands all day long
to stubborn people.*

In the face of tragedy, people often point to the suffering as evidence of God's so-called aloofness. If God were concerned about human beings, the argument goes, he wouldn't allow such disasters to occur. Yet all biblical evidence suggests that just the opposite is true. God is vitally concerned about every aspect of our lives. It is human beings who demonstrate indifference toward God. If it seems like the height of presumption for humans to ignore God, consider this: God, in his unfathomable patience, continues to wait for people to turn to him. Actions that deserve eternal judgment are not punished immediately. Instead God chooses to wait patiently for people to seek him.

A Moment with God

Thank God for the fact that he chose to wait for you even while you weren't seeking him.

For Further Reading:
Isaiah 65:1-25

Rescue!

Jeremiah 1:7-8—But the LORD said to me, "Don't say that you are only a boy. You will go wherever I send you. You will say whatever I command you to say. Don't be afraid of people. I am with you, and I will rescue you."

A Moment with God

Have you ever needed God to rescue you? What were the circumstances? Can you use that experience to be a witness for this facet of God?

For Further Reading: Jeremiah 1:4-10

*H*ave you ever seen a lost child at the mall? If you have, you can't forget the look of panic in the eyes, the tension in the fingers, the anxiety in the fidgets. Have you seen a lost child reunited with her parent? The parent reassures the child, telling her that all is well, that he won't let go of her again, that she can depend on him. From that point on, the child remembers: If I'm ever lost again, my mom or dad will come and find me. That's the assurance we have from our heavenly father, too. Regardless of the circumstances, no matter how far from him we drift, he wants nothing more than to rescue his children.

The Boiling Point

Jeremiah 7:16, 19—
"Jeremiah, don't
pray for these
people. Don't cry or
pray for them.
. . . They aren't
really provoking
me," declares the
LORD. "But they are
harming them-
selves to their own
shame."

G od's anger is not like that of a mother at 6:00 who, with dinner on the stove and a meeting to get to by 6:30, finally has enough of her arguing children and blows her stack just as the beans are boiling over. God's anger is not blinded by feelings or preoccupied with other matters—a short fuse waiting to be ignited. Instead, his anger is laced with compassion: not worrying about how our offenses have hurt his feelings but how foolishly we rebel against his word—teachings that are not meant to spoil our fun but to keep us from creating our own harm.

A Moment with God

God can protect us from the trouble our fun can get us into.

For Further Reading:
Jeremiah 7:1-26

God's 911

*Jeremiah 15:20—
I will make you
like a solid bronze
wall in front of
these people. They
will fight you, but
they will not defeat
you. I am with you,
and I will save you
and rescue you,
declares the LORD.*

A Moment with God

What situation are
you in today? Thank
God for being there
with you. Always
remember he is only
a call away.

*For Further Reading:
Jeremiah 15:1-21*

*M*any small children have saved
a family member from death by
dialing 911. They knew what
they had to do to get help in an
emergency.

God is on 24-hour emergency
call for us. His line is never busy.
When we call, he is quick to
rescue us. God never hides from
us or goes on vacation. He is an
attentive parent who will brave
any danger and pay any price to
keep us safe.

Our worst moments are
when we think we are alone in
our troubles. Our enemy tries to
convince us God doesn't care or
can't help. It simply isn't true.
God loves us so much he will be
with us in every situation.

Someone to Trust

*Jeremiah 17:7—
Blessed is the
person who trusts
the LORD. The LORD
will be his
confidence.*

*I*s there anyone whom you trust
unreservedly? Your spouse, a
best friend, a sister? As a child,
you probably trusted your
parents that way . . . until they
failed you. As an adult you may
choose to trust someone, but
you've learned from experience
that you'll be disappointed at
some point. Humans fail. However, there is someone whom
you can trust who will never fail
you. God is completely trustworthy. He always keeps his word,
he never violates a confidence,
he always wants the best for you.
Don't judge God by human
standards. He is one you can
trust with everything you are.
You won't be disappointed.

A Moment with God

God will never fail
you! Praise him for
his trustworthiness.

*For Further Reading:
Jeremiah 17:5-11*

Near or Far, but Never Gone

JULY 31

*Jeremiah 23:23—
"I am a God who is
near. I am also a
God who is far
away," declares the
LORD.*

*T*he existence of a relationship is not determined by proximity. Whether you are near or far away from your family does not affect the fact that a family bond exists. What is affected is the enjoyment of that relationship, how much the relationship is enjoyed. It is much the same with God. God sometimes seems as near as our own breath and at other times as unreachable as the stars. There are two things to remember when there is distance between you and God. First, remind yourself that *far* is not the same as *gone*. Then, since God never changes, think about who moved.

A Moment with God

Consider what it is in your life that puts distance between you and God. Praise him for being constant, always there even when it doesn't feel like it.

*For Further Reading:
Jeremiah 23:16-24*

God Has Plans for You

AUGUST 1

Jeremiah 29:11— I know the plans that I have for you, declares the LORD. They are plans for peace and not disaster, plans to give you a future filled with hope.

God wishes his children well. He dreams big dreams for them. He sticks close and protects them. He gives them hope. Whether he is speaking to captives in Old Testament Babylon or the late twentieth century, he gives hope for what he will bring about. Whether he is speaking to captives of enemy nations or captives of unhappiness and greed, he gives hope for freedom. He gives hope for the final outcome. He gives hope beyond whatever current circumstances may be. God gives his children hope for the better plans he has for them.

A Moment with God

Talk to God about the places where you feel hopeless.

For Further Reading: Jeremiah 29:4-14

Just Call

Jeremiah 33:3—
Call to me, and I
will answer you. I
will tell you great
and mysterious
things that you
do not know.

A Moment with God

Praise God for his open heart, which invites us to call him anytime, and promises to answer us.

For Further Reading:
Jeremiah 33:1-11

What would you do if the mayor of your town or the governor of your state or the president of the United States said to you, "Look, call me, anytime. I'll be there to take your call"? It would feel pretty amazing, wouldn't it? Yet that is exactly what the Lord of the universe says to us. In fact, God's invitation to call on him comes with a promise: "Call to me, and I will answer you." What an amazing reality. God doesn't say, "You can try to call me, and if I'm up to it, I'll listen." No. He says, "Just call. Tell me your joys, sorrows, concerns, and questions. I will listen, and I will answer."

Promises

*Jeremiah 35:15—
I have sent all my
servants the
prophets to you
again and again.
They said, "Turn
from your evil
ways, do what is
right, and don't
follow other gods
in order to serve
them."*

God has expectations. He has
given us directions, commands,
and promises. This verse summa-
rizes three specific divine require-
ments: repentance, right living,
and trust in the one true God.

God has repeatedly made his
will known. He promised that good
would flow from obedience. Yet
people have failed miserably. We
have ignored and resisted God's
instructions. We have treated God
lightly. Biblical history is full of
examples of people God didn't have
to punish because they suffered the
horrible but inevitable consequences of their own choices. Be a
person who learns from these
examples. Ask God for his help in
living up to his expectations.

A Moment with God

Ask the Lord to help
you think twice
before neglecting any
expectations he
makes known to you.

*For Further Reading:
Jeremiah 35:1-19*

As Good As His Word

*Jeremiah 39:17-18—
But at that time I
will rescue you,
declares the LORD.
You will not be
handed over to
those you fear. I
will certainly
rescue you. You
will not die in
war. You will
escape with your
life because you
trusted me.*

A Moment with God

Think of as many
promises in Scripture
as you can.
Thank God for the
assurance that
every one of those
promises will be
fulfilled.

*For Further Reading:
Jeremiah 39:1-18*

Once upon a time, a person's
word was legally binding. All
business transactions and legal
proceedings were finalized with
nothing more concrete than a
handshake. Today, even the
most basic agreements require
contracts, receipts, and even
lawyers. As a result, the value of
a person's word has decreased
sharply. God's word, however,
remains as unassailable today as
it was in biblical times. Those
who God promises to protect can
rest assured that God will not
allow them to be harmed.

Good Versus Evil

Jeremiah 51:56—A destroyer will attack Babylon, its soldiers will be captured, and their bows and arrows will be broken. "I, the LORD, am a God who punishes evil. I will certainly punish them."

God doesn't just look the other way when evil approaches. He goes into action. He doesn't just turn a deaf ear to evil. He turns off the volume. God doesn't just dislike evil. God despises evil. The simple, undeniable fact is that God cannot tolerate rampant evil and disobedience. Goodness and evil cannot abide together, and since God is good, nearness to evil is not an option. The natural consequence of evil is destruction. That's the message the prophet Jeremiah tried to convey to Judah and the surrounding nations: stop sinning or be destroyed.

A Moment with God

Contemplate the nature of God and his goodness. Consider the reasons why good and evil are incompatible.

For Further Reading: Jeremiah 51:56-64

Spared!

Lamentations 3:21-23—
"The reason I can still find hope is that I keep this one thing in mind: the LORD's mercy. We were not completely wiped out.
His compassion is never limited.
It is new every morning. His faithfulness is great."

A Moment with God

Thank God again and again for sparing you from the full consequences of your sin.

For Further Reading: Lamentations 3:21-41

Life is full of consequences. When we lie, trust is destroyed; when we cheat, people get hurt; when we gossip, relationships are ruined. However tough the consequences of our sins, though, we don't ever get the full punishment we deserve. Our God is overwhelmingly merciful. We deserve death for our sin, yet he pardons us. We deserve to be completely cut off from God, yet he still pursues a relationship with us. When you blow it, don't despair. Take hope in the fact that the painful results are only a taste of what could have been yours; our God will continue to show you compassion and mercy. He loves you that much.

Unexpected Splendor

Ezekiel 1:28—
The brightness all
around him looked
like a rainbow in
the clouds. It was
like the LORD's
glory. When I saw
it, I immediately
bowed down, and I
heard someone
speaking.

God sometimes has a way of showing up when we least expect it. He casts his love across the sky in a blazing summer sunset. He whispers to us softly through the sweet melodies of a solo in Sunday's morning worship service. He touches our hands with the wet nose of a newborn pup. He shouts his presence on a moonlit, star-filled evening. God reveals his glory to us unexpectedly to get our attention. He reminds us that he still exists. He wants us to know that he is still in control. He wants us to be still for a moment and know that he alone is God.

A Moment with God

Thank God for the many wonderful ways that he reveals himself to you in the world around you.

For Further Reading:
Ezekiel 1:1-28

No God but Me

*Ezekiel 6:9b—
I was hurt by their
adulterous hearts,
which turned away
from me, and by
their eyes, which
lusted after idols.
They will hate
themselves for the
evil and disgusting
things that they
have done.*

A Moment with God

List the qualities of
God that set him
apart from false
gods. Praise God for
his greatness and
power.

*For Further Reading:
Ezekiel 6:1-14*

God insists on our complete
loyalty and commitment. He is a
jealous God who doesn't want to
share worship with false gods.
Most often we think of jealousy
as a negative trait. It describes a
person who feels insecure and
tries to control another person's
relationships out of selfishness.

God's jealousy is nothing like
human jealousy or envy. He calls
his people to worship and honor
him alone because he is the one,
true God. No one else can match
his power and greatness. His
holiness demands our undivided
allegiance.

Whatever the Price

AUGUST 9

Ezekiel 12:15—
Then they will
know that I am the
LORD, because I
will scatter them
among the nations
and force them into
other countries.

God spares no expense in refining his people. If their rebellion requires unpleasantness, he would rather be unpleasant than lose that relationship. God doesn't just want his people happy—he wants them righteous and devoted to him. And he is willing to pay a great price to keep them that way. He proved that in plagues. He proved that in the desert. He proved that on the cross. He will not sit idly as his people wander away, no matter what it costs.

A Moment with God

Ask God to draw you to him today—then be ready for whatever he has for you.

For Further Reading:
Ezekiel 12:14-20

221

Waiting on Words from You

*Ezekiel 22:30—
I looked for
someone among you
who could build
walls or stand in
front of me by the
gaps in the walls to
defend the land and
keep it from being
destroyed. But I
couldn't find
anyone.*

A Moment with God

Take advantage of
prayer today. Pray
for yourself, your
friends, and your
family.

*For Further Reading:
Ezekiel 22:1-31*

*T*he Bible is proof that God's
anger can burn hot against the
sins of his people. Yet he honors
us with the undeserved privilege
of listening to our cries for
mercy. In prayer, he not only
gives us the ability to speak but
the confidence that we are being
heard—that our appeals are not
falling on deaf ears but are being
registered in heavenly places.
The all-knowing God, who sees
to the heart of every action, is
still willing to give us a second
chance. He takes no delight in
people's ruin but longs for them
to turn their faces toward his.
Again. And again. And again.

Harvest

God has revealed himself in many ways: the word, creation, Jesus Christ. He also chose a people to call his own. He promised to make them his representatives in the world. Against all odds and in spite of repeated extermination campaigns, the people of Israel have survived.

As the Bible demonstrates, the ultimate fate of the Jewish nation has never been in human hands. God did not choose them for their qualities. He wanted a people through whom he could demonstrate his own holiness to the world. Israel survives as a testimony of God's character. The world continues to be amazed that God keeps his promises.

AUGUST 11

Ezekiel 28:25—This is what the Almighty LORD says: When I gather the people of Israel from the nations where they were scattered, I will show that I am holy as the nations watch. The people of Israel will live in their own land.

A Moment with God

Lord, continue to show your holiness to the world as the history of your people unfolds.

For Further Reading: Ezekiel 28:20-26

The Judge

*Ezekiel 33:11—
As I live, declares
the Almighty
LORD, I don't want
wicked people to
die. Rather, I want
them to turn from
their ways and
live. Change the
way you think and
act! Turn from
your wicked ways!*

A Moment with God

Consider the mercy
that God has shown
you, giving you an
opportunity to repent
of your "capital
offense" of sin and
withholding his
judgment from you

*For Further Reading:
Ezekiel 33:1-33*

One of the most notorious figures
of the Old West was the "hanging
judge." A hanging judge was a
justice of the peace known for his
hasty death sentences. Accused
murderers, horse thieves, cattle
rustlers, and even some card
cheats stood very little chance
when they were brought before a
hanging judge.

If any arbiter of justice had
the right to be a hanging judge, it
is God. All sin is direct disobedience to God's word. Yet rather
than impose swift and sure
punishment, God gives us
opportunities to repent and turn
to him. Praise God that he
withholds the "death penalty"
from those who look to him for
salvation. Praise him for the
salvation he has given you.

God's Righteous Standards

Ezekiel 45:9—
This is what the
Almighty LORD
says: I've had
enough of you, you
princes of Israel.
Stop your violence
and looting, and
do what is fair
and right.

*I*f asked to define God's righteousness, most of us would probably say that God cannot sin. But it really goes a step further— because he is righteous and cannot sin, he has no tolerance for sin. God not only abides by his moral law, he requires it of his people, too. Our righteous God doesn't have different standards for what is right in different situations, and he expects the same of us. Cheating is sin, whether it's cheating on a spouse, income taxes, or a customer. Stealing is wrong whether it's stealing from God by not giving him his due or from an employer by "borrowing" office supplies. Even the smallest details matter to God. His righteousness can't be compromised; it is all or nothing.

A Moment with God

Do you use God's standards for righteous living? Ask him to help you do so.

For Further Reading:
Ezekiel 45:9-16

Light and Truth

*Daniel 2:21b-22—
He gives wisdom to
those who are wise
and knowledge to
those who have
insight. He reveals
deeply hidden
things. He knows
what is in the
dark, and light
lives with him.*

A Moment with God

God's light is available to you today and able to shine in you and through you. Thank him for this marvelous truth.

*For Further Reading
Daniel 2:16-22*

There is a light that lives in God that goes far beyond the physical. It penetrates our very soul and reveals what lies deeply hidden in us, lurking in the darkness of our own personal closet. There is nothing so deeply hidden, so completely buried in the dark, that the light of God cannot reveal it. Pay attention to the verbs in these two verses. What does the light that lives with God do? The light that resides with God reveals, knows, and lives. Revealing leads to really knowing, and it is only by knowing, really knowing, that we will ever really live.

Creative Genius

*Daniel 4:2—
I am pleased to
write to you about
the miraculous
signs and amazing
things the Most
High God did
for me.*

*I*t's a high-tech world we live in—
millisecond communication,
satellites spying on satellites
spying on other satellites, and
computer-smart kids who can use
a keyboard before they can talk.
Amazing, isn't it? Even more
amazing, though, is the power of
God. Can we compare the
intellect that invents a laser beam
to the intellect that designed a
heart? Is a fax machine more
awesome than a sunset? What an
incredible force is our God! What
a creative genius!

A Moment with God

List some of the
everyday things that
God created.
Consider how they
bless your life.

*For Further Reading:
Daniel 4:1-37*

Forgiving the Rebellious

*Daniel 9:9—
But you, Lord our
God, are compas-
sionate and
forgiving, although
we have rebelled
against you.*

A Moment with God

Thank God for his
patience and mercy
in loving and
forgiving you, even
though you are
rebellious.

*For Further Reading:
Daniel 9:4-23*

We don't like to admit that we
are rebellious people, but we
are. Caught up in the spirit of
our age, we like to do things *our
way.* We rebel when people try
to tell us what to do. We rebel
even against God and his word.
But God has good new for us.
He is compassionate and forgiving, even though we have
rebelled against him. If we
confess to God that we have
been selfish, stubborn, and
rebellious in trying to live
without concern for him or his
word, he will forgive us and give
us another chance.

Jilted Lover

*Hosea 2:14—
That is why I'm
going to win her
back. I will lead
her into the desert.
I will speak
tenderly to her.*

God's message to his people through Hosea was sexually graphic. Every time Hosea's wife cheated on him, God reminded the people that they had forsaken him and sought immoral pleasure and false gods. Remarkably, God's response as a jilted husband is not revenge. God sent Hosea searching diligently for Gomer—the same way God comes looking for us.

God's love for you is never ending. When you wander away, he actively seeks to win you back. God is constantly trying to woo you back to him with tender messages of love.

A Moment with God

No one looks for God as intently as God looks for them. Thank God for his unlimited, unconditional love for you.

*For Further Reading:
Hosea 2:14-23*

229

Search for God

Hosea 5:15—
I will go back to
my place until they
admit that they are
guilty. Then they
will search for me.
In their distress
they will eagerly
look for me.

A Moment with God

Ask God to give you a great appetite for his presence.

For Further Reading:
Hosea 5:1-15

God loves his people and wants to be in close relationship to them. He wants his presence to be welcome. He wants his company to be sought after. God should be an honored guest at our table, a cherished one among us. But God will not join with us if we are full of sin. He waits for us to admit our sins and respond to him appropriately. He waits for us to realize just how serious our error has been. He waits for us to eagerly search him out.

Breaking Out of a Rut

Hosea 6:6—
I want your
loyalty, not your
sacrifices. I want
you to know me,
not to give me
burnt offerings.

*D*o you ever feel like you are in a rut? You wake up, go to work, come home, plan dinner, take the kids to activities, work on the yard, collapse in bed, and start all over. Church can be the same dull routine if you are not careful. You wake up, go to church, sit in a pew, listen to some songs and a sermon, and go home. God never intended that. He doesn't want ritualistic church attendance—he wants a relationship with you. He wants to walk with you and talk with you during your week. When God is in your day, there is never a dull moment.

A Moment with God

Praise God for his desire to spend time with you. Thank him for choosing to have a relationship with you.

For Further Reading:
Hosea 6:1-11

Waiting to Forgive

*Hosea 14:2—
Return to the LORD,
and say these things
to him: "Forgive all
our sins, and kindly
receive us. Then
we'll praise you
with our lips."*

A Moment with God

Do you have any unconfessed sins in your life? Bring them to God now. Ask for his merciful forgiveness.

For Further Reading: Hosea 14:1-9

*T*here is reason to be awed at the magnitude of God's forgiveness. It's not a grudging, "Oh, all right, I'll forgive you." Nor is it, "I'll forgive you, but things just won't be the same between us." It's not even, "OK, but if you blow it again, you're outta here!" The wonder of his forgiveness is that he is eager and waiting to forgive us the moment we repent and ask him to. Then he restores our relationship with him, lavishing his love and good gifts on us. Finally, he works in our lives to help us mature so we won't continue to commit such sins. The incredible scope of such forgiveness is certainly not humanly possible; it is, thank God, divinely so!

An Outpouring

Joel 2:28—
After this, I will
pour my Spirit on
everyone. Your
sons and daugh-
ters will prophesy.
Your old men will
dream dreams.
Your young men
will see visions.

*H*undreds of years after Joel penned these words, a tiny band of Jesus' followers saw the prophecy come true at Pentecost. Peter used this exact passage to explain to the crowds what had suddenly happened to the disciples (Acts 2:1-21). On the night before his arrest, Jesus had prepared his followers for this central result of his own victory over death and sin (John 14:15-25). The Holy Spirit would indwell believers. He would "work" on everyone.

Look at it this way. Everyone you meet today will be under the influence of the Holy Spirit. Some will be responding; others resisting. And that same Spirit will be active in you.

A Moment with God

Ask God to give you a special glimpse of how the Holy Spirit works in various people today.

For Further Reading:
Joel 2:18-31

Unlikely Christians

Joel 2:32—
Then whoever calls
on the name of the
LORD will be saved.
Those who escape
will be on Mount
Zion and in
Jerusalem. Among
the survivors will
be those whom the
LORD calls, as the
LORD has promised.

A Moment with God

Praise God for the fact that his salvation is available to everyone. Then start a list of the names of people with whom you'd like to share the message of God's salvation.

For Further Reading:
Joel 2:32–3:21

The history of Christianity records countless examples of unlikely conversions. Perhaps the most dramatic conversion in all the New Testament is that of Saul, the Jewish zealot who persecuted and killed the early Christians. After a personal encounter with Christ, this enemy of Christianity became one of the most important figures in the early church—the apostle Paul. You probably know or have heard of others whose lives were radically changed when they became Christians. Fortunately for us, no one is ever too far gone to receive God's salvation. Whoever calls upon the name of the Lord will be saved.

Roar Again, Lord!

Just as in this verse, often in Scripture we see the imagery of God as the Lion of Judah. A roaring, thundering lion is equated with powerful, mighty God. Yet whenever this image is employed, the lion is seen not as a destroyer or killer of weaker creatures. Instead, the lion is used to illustrate power. Rather than a negative, fearsome image, the metaphor of God as lion is a reminder of his strength to help his children, his authority to defend his children, and his majestic presence on the plain of our lives.

AUGUST 23

Amos 1:2—
He said: The LORD
roars from Zion,
and his voice
thunders from
Jerusalem. The
pastures of the
shepherds are
turning brown,
and the top of
ₗMountₗ Carmel is
dried up.

A Moment with God

Ask God to be a lion for you. Ask him to roar against forces that might harm you.

For Further Reading:
Amos 1:1-15

What the Heavens Declare

Amos 5:8—
God made the
⌊constellations⌋
Pleiades and
Orion. He turns
deep darkness into
dawn. He turns
day into night. He
calls for water
from the sea to
pour it over the
face of the earth.
His name is the
LORD.

A Moment with God

Lose yourself in the awesome timelessness of God, and let his record of faithfulness give you confidence for today.

For Further Reading:
Amos 5:4-17

When you read Amos's writings and hear him testify how God made clusters of stars that we can still—thousands of years later—go out under a night time sky and see with our own two eyes. It is as if God suddenly becomes as close as our front yard. To think that God has always been and will always be, that he has been communing with his people under the clear sky for longer than our imaginations can dream, proves that his promises will stand the test of time. In fact, they already have.

The Most Powerful Name

G God can do what men and
women can only dream of doing.
He controls the earth and the
heavens. Everything created is
under his domination and power.
While recent discoveries and
advances in medicine and
technology suggest that scien-
tists will try to be like God by
controlling life, these scientific
breakthroughs reveal a deeper
awareness of the awesome
power and work of God. The size
and complexity of our world
begs for science to look for a
master creator. All explanations
that leave out God are inadequate and shortsighted. All we
know could be instantly snuffed
out by a command from God.
His power is beyond measure or
description. It is a mighty God
we serve.

AUGUST 25

*Amos 9:5—
The Almighty
Lord of Armies
touches the earth.
It quakes, and all
who live on it
mourn.*

A Moment with God

Walk through your
world today looking
for the handiwork of
God. Praise him for
his infinite power to
create such beauty
and such a
magnificent world.

*For Further Reading:
Amos 9:1-15*

The Toughest Love

*Obadiah 1:4—
"Even though you
fly high like an
eagle and build
your nest among
the stars, I will
bring you down
from there,"
declares the LORD.*

A Moment with God

Humble yourself and
confess your sin.

*For Further Reading:
Obadiah 1:1-14*

God loves. God forgives. God shows patience. He gives second chances. God weeps. God grieves. God calls his children back. He does everything he can to correct their paths.

And then he becomes their judge. He calls black, black and white, white. He reveals their sins and shows where they have fallen short of his standards. And when his gavel falls, it is with swift conviction.

He offers a choice between salvation and destruction and then meets each choice as Savior or judge.

You Can't Ignore God

*Jonah 1:3—
Jonah immediately
tried to run away
from the LORD by
going to Tarshish.
He went to Joppa
and found a ship
going to Tarshish.
He paid for the
trip and went on
board. He wanted
to go to Tarshish
to get away from
the LORD.*

*I*f God has given you instructions and you're doing your best
to ignore them, be advised! You
cannot ignore God for very long.
You can't hide from him—he's
everywhere. No excuse will
suffice if he's asking you to
become involved in his work.
God's agenda is not limited by
your attempts to "run away," for
he is all powerful. He will pursue
you; he will do things to get your
attention till you join his team.
Though he can accomplish
anything without you, he loves
you enough to want you to be
involved in the wonder of his work.

A Moment with God

Are you avoiding
God's call in some
area of your life?
Confess your
reluctance to him,
then get moving!

*For Further Reading:
Jonah 1:1–2:10*

Three-D Love

*Jonah 4:2b—
I knew that you
are a merciful and
compassionate
God, patient, and
always ready to
forgive and to
reconsider your
threats of
destruction.*

A Moment with God

Think of a situation in your life where you have experienced God's forgiveness. Then look in it for elements of his great compassion, patience, and mercy.

For Further Reading: Jonah 3:1–4:3

*M*ercy, compassion, patience, forgiveness. This grouping of qualities remains forever linked. One is almost unthinkable without the other. Just try to define one without using the other. It simply doesn't work. How can one describe forgiveness without talking about mercy? If one speaks of compassion without mentioning patience, the full meaning just doesn't come across. It is like looking at something only in one dimension. As with everything real in this world, the compassion of God is distinctly three dimensional. It looks different from every angle.

God Will Punish Evil

AUGUST 29

Micah 3:8—
But I am filled
with the power of
the LORD's Spirit,
with justice, and
with strength.
So I will tell ⌐the
descendants of⌐
Jacob about their
crimes and ⌐the
nation of⌐Israel
about its sins.

God's character includes both his mercy and his justice. While his mercy demands that he be long-suffering and patient with our stubbornness, his justice demands that he punish evil. God told the Old Testament prophets to warn the people that, if they continued to disregard his laws and will, he would punish them. And true to his word, he did. We need to have a healthy respect for God's justice. He will not only punish unrepentant sin in our lives but also punish the evil that seems to go unchecked in our world. When human laws and systems fail to punish unspeakable evil, we can count on God's justice to punish the evildoers.

A Moment with God

Confess your own sin to God, then thank him for his justice.

For Further Reading:
Micah 3:1-12

Tiny Town

Micah 5:2—
You, Bethlehem
Ephrathah, are
too small to be
included among
Judah's cities. Yet,
from you Israel's
future ruler will
come for me. His
origins go back to
the distant past, to
days long ago.

A Moment with God

Don't place limits on God by overemphasizing your shortcomings while minimizing the Lord's infinite power.

For Further Reading: Micah 5:2-4

These dusty travelers in Jerusalem created quite a stir. These "wise men" were looking for a newborn king! They were not asking *if* a king had been born. Of that they were sure. They just wanted directions to his home.

The religious leaders were consulted about any prophesied locations for a royal birth. Their answer was immediate. The little town of Bethlehem had been identified as the birthplace of the future great and promised king.

God has never allowed the size, reputation, or importance of places or people to determine their usefulness. God can still do something very special with who you are, where you find yourself right now.

The Art of Forgiveness

Micah 7:18-19—Who is a God like you? You forgive sin and overlook the rebellion of your faithful people. You will not be angry forever, because you would rather show mercy. You will again have compassion on us.

*I*n the Lord's Prayer, Jesus instructs his disciples to ask God to "forgive us as we forgive others" (Matthew 6:12). The model of forgiveness that God provides for believers is complete amnesia. Because of his great compassion for us, God throws every one of our confessed sins into the deepest sea, never to consider them again. God chooses to completely forget about our offenses against him—if we simply repent and ask forgiveness for them.

How well do you follow God's example in forgiving people who have wronged you?

A Moment with God

Thank God for the fact that he chooses not to remember your sins. Consider how you might follow his model of forgiveness in your dealings with others.

For Further Reading:
Micah 7:1-20

243

A Ray of Hope

Nahum 1:7—
The LORD is good.
⌊He is⌋ a fortress in
the day of trouble.
He knows those who
seek shelter in him.

A Moment with God

Have you fled to God in times of trouble? Remember Nahum's call for hope.

For Further Reading:
Nahum 1:1-14

The little book of Nahum has a singular purpose: to report the prophet's vision of the destruction of Ninevah. Line by line, Ninevah is warned of the terrors to come—of God's anger and might and unceasing rage toward disobedience. What does that have to do with the goodness of God? It makes God's people alert to signs of God's goodness, and if we look closely, we'll find it. In the midst of this frightening report of impending doom, there it is, one ray of hope: The Lord is good. God is a shelter, reminds Nahum, for those who seek him. Not only does God provide refuge, but he warns any who would harm his refugees: I know my children.

244

For Better or For Worse

The gray skies overhead may have hidden the sun for weeks. Your checking account may be empty, and your car may be on the blink. Bills could be stacked high, and the refrigerator could be empty. Perhaps you are broke, or maybe your health has not been good. Perhaps your life is a mess with no sign of rest. What do you do? Habakkuk did the exact opposite of what most people would do. He rested in God's peace and decided he would be happy, even if he had nothing. God's peace is available to you even when nothing else is. True peace comes from God, not from circumstances.

SEPTEMBER 2

Habakkuk 3:17b-18—Even if the olive tree fails to produce and the fields yield no food, even if the sheep pen is empty and the stalls have no cattle— even then, I will be happy with the LORD. I will truly find joy in God, who saves me.

A Moment with God

Pray that God will help you find your peace in his loving arms, not from the circumstances around you.

For Further Reading: Habakkuk 3:1-19

God's Joyful Shout

*Zephaniah 3:17—
The LORD your God
is with you. He is a
hero who saves
you. He happily
rejoices over you,
renews you with
his love, and
celebrates over you
with shouts of joy.*

A Moment with God

Reflect on the
wonder of God's
mercy. Praise God
for being merciful
to you.

*For Further Reading:
Zephaniah 3:14-17*

*I*t is a sad reality that we all
deserve God's judgment in our
lifetime. We're all sinners living
in a fallen world. But there is
hope. We know a time will come
when God in his mercy will
reverse his judgment against us.
He will save us from our sinful
selves. He will restore our
relationship with him. And, as
excited as that knowledge makes
us, God is more excited, more
joyful over that prospect than we
are. Only he can fully understand how incredibly lost we are;
only he can fully appreciate the
wonder of the new life he gives
us. How amazing that he shouts
for joy over our rescue! How
much he must love us!

I Am with You!

Use your imagination to place yourself in a situation that would frighten you, such as hiking alone in a dark woods, hearing your job was being eliminated, or lying in a hospital bed waiting for surgery. Where could you find help and strength to match those challenges? The refugees who returned to Jerusalem thought God had forgotten them. God sent his prophet to remind the people that he was right beside them as they faced trouble.

When God allows difficulties and problems to discipline us, it is easy to feel like God is far away and disinterested in us. In reality God has not forgotten us. He is still close by, ready and willing to encourage us and available to help us with our problems.

SEPTEMBER 4
*Haggai 2:4-5—
"But now, Zerubbabel, be strong," declares the LORD. "Chief Priest Joshua, . . . be strong. Everyone in the land, be strong," declares the LORD. "Work, because I am with you," declares the LORD of Armies.*

A Moment with God

Tell God about the situations that keep you awake at night. Ask him to help you trust him.

For Further Reading: Haggai 2:1-9

What Does a Loving God Hate?

SEPTEMBER 5

*Zechariah 8:17—
Don't even think
of doing evil to
each other. Don't
enjoy false
testimony. I hate
all these things,
declares the LORD.*

God hates sin. He doesn't just get offended by it. He doesn't just think it unpleasant. He wouldn't just rather us do something else. He hates sin. He hates all that has to do with sin. He hates everything it stands for. He cannot abide with it. He would rather us be unhappy than full of sin. Over and over he has provided ways for his people to be cleansed from sin. He hates its stench. He hates its lure. He hates its final outcome. And he would rather die himself than have us live in it.

A Moment with God

Take time to evaluate what habits you have that do not honor God.

*For Further Reading:
Zechariah 8:14-17*

Hope on the Horizon

*Zechariah 10:6—
I will strengthen
the people of
Judah. I will rescue
Joseph's people. I
will bring them
back, because I
have compassion
for them. It will be
as though I had
never rejected
them, because I am
the LORD their God.*

*M*uch of the prophets' writings
are harsh and condemning—and
rightly so—for the rebellion of
God's people and their forgetful-
ness of his favor were as serious
then as they are today. Yet amid
the most dire and disastrous of
times, God always weaves a
pattern of hope: Hope that he
will not leave you to drift de-
fenselessly into ruin, that he will
welcome you with open arms
and call the dogs of discipline off
your weary soul if you'll only
return to your first love—your
only hope for deliverance.

A Moment with God

Today may find you in
a hopeless place, but
God can give you
enough hope to make
it till tomorrow.

*For Further Reading:
Zechariah 10:6-12*

Giving

*Malachi 3:10—
"Bring one-tenth of
your income into
the storehouse so
that there may be
food in my house.
Test me in this
way," says the
LORD of Armies.
"See if I won't
open the windows
of heaven for you
and flood you with
blessings."*

A Moment with God

Have you prayerfully
considered how
much trust your
patterns of giving
express toward God?

*For Further Reading:
Malachi 3:6-18*

How easily we forget that God
has dared us to trust him. This
verse even invites us to "test"
him. God laid out some specific
terms for the experiment: We
give back to him some of what
he has given us and then expect
him to more than make up for
what we have presented.

Since God has not changed,
the same conditions are still in
place. Unfortunately, most of us
give out of duty or guilt. Giving
what's left over has little to do with
trust. Returning as much as a
tenth to the Lord as a first priority
immediately makes life adventure-
some. Clear acts of trust will
increase anyone's awareness of
God's trustworthiness.

I Predict

SEPTEMBER 8

*Matthew 1:23—
"The virgin will
become pregnant
and give birth to a
son, and they will
name him
Immanuel," which
means "God is
with us."*

*A*t the end of the year, tabloid
newspapers usually publish their
psychic predictions for the
coming year. The premiere
source for predictions and
prophecies, of course, is the
Bible. Jesus Christ himself
fulfilled hundreds of Old Testament prophecies concerning the
Messiah. Unlike tabloid predictions or psychic hotline readings, the prophecies of Scripture
can be fully trusted. We can
know that Christ will indeed
return, as is prophesied in
Scripture. We can be sure that
he will set up his foretold
kingdom on earth. God, in his
perfection, has fulfilled—or will
fulfill—every prophecy of the
Bible.

A Moment with God

Praise God for the
perfection of his
biblical prophecies.
Thank him for the
assurance that every
prediction in Scripture
will be fulfilled.

*For Further Reading:
Matthew 1:1-25*

The House of Quiet

*Matthew 5:12—
Rejoice and be
glad because you
have a great
reward in heaven!
The prophets who
lived before you
were persecuted in
these ways.*

A Moment with God

Is there someone with whom you need to make peace? Ask God to give you the courage to do so. Today!

*For Further Reading:
Matthew 5:1-48*

*T*here aren't too many fathers who enjoy seeing their children fighting, are there? There aren't too many dads who want their home filled with arguing, bickering children whose rivalry makes home a war zone. Most fathers want peace, especially among their children. A home of peace, a house of quiet, where love abounds: this is the desire of most dads. And God is like that, too. He honors peace because he is the God of Peace. Even when Scripture tells us he disciplined his people, the action grew out of God's desire for peace—peace among his children or peace between God and his people.

Reason to Worry?

SEPTEMBER 10

Matthew 6:26— Look at the birds. They don't plant, harvest, or gather the harvest into barns. Yet, your heavenly Father feeds them. Aren't you worth more than they?

What could be more natural than worry? If you are human, sooner or later, hardship strikes. We are so aware of the possibility of calamity that we have come to anticipate it long before it happens. Often the focus of our worry never happens at all. As understandable as anxiety may seem to us, Jesus insisted that it was unproductive, even illogical. The Father who cares for the birds that glide through the air cares for us! The God who clothes the grass of the fields places much greater value on us. Every minute detail of our lives is held in his loving hands. What, then, can worry add?

A Moment with God

Imagine! The God of creation cares for your tiniest detail!

For Further Reading: Matthew 6:25-34

How Much More

*Matthew 7:9—
If your child asks
you for bread,
would any of you
give him a stone?*

A Moment with God

Praise God that his
goodness often goes
beyond what we can
understand.

*For Further Reading:
Matthew 7:7-14*

*E*ver try to explain to a struggling
two-year-old that the shot he is
about to get is really an act of love
on the part of his parents? Don't
bother; it doesn't work! The child
can't believe that any benefit is
worth the pain he's about to
receive. But parents know that
the pain is temporary and the
benefits will last a lifetime. To the
child, the shot is painful. To the
parent, the shot is security.

In a similar way, God can
seem cruel or loving, depending
on our point of view. We spend so
much of our lives looking through
the eyes of that struggling two-
year-old. We see fear, and we see
pain, and we see a needle coming.
What we don't see is the goodness and the love and the face of
the Father on the other side of
the needle.

Creation Obeys Jesus

SEPTEMBER 12

Matthew 8:26—Jesus said to them, "Why do you cowards have so little faith?" Then he got up, gave an order to the wind and the sea, and the sea became very calm.

When we have a hard time trusting God's power, we need only read this story to have a graphic reminder that we can—and must—trust him. In the middle of his disciples' fear of the threatening storm, Jesus merely gives the order, he merely speaks a word, and the gale quiets to complete calm. If God can calm the furious storm on the lake, he can calm the raging storms of fear, uncertainty, pain, bitterness, and loneliness in our hearts as well. Allow him to speak his words of peace into our storms. Have the courage to believe that he can and will calm the storm.

A Moment with God

Trusting that God still has the power to make even the winds and waves obey him, give him your personal storms.

For Further Reading: Matthew 8:23-32

255

Share the Load

*Matthew 11:28—
Come to me, all
who are tired from
carrying heavy
loads, and I will
give you rest.*

God cares. While some people curse God in moments of disappointment, we can be confident that God understands our needs. God knows life is difficult. Jesus acknowledged that being tired from carrying heavy loads is normal. God knows what we are going through and how much we can handle.

God invites us to come to him in our exhaustion and share the load with him. He wants to put his shoulder under our load and help us push on. Jesus was clear in reminding us that we have a standing offer of help from the king of heaven. God does care.

A Moment with God

Whatever burdens you are facing right now, God offers his help and his rest to you. You don't have to fight your battles alone. God promises to be by your side.

*For Further Reading:
Matthew 11:20-30*

Could You Recognize God?

*Matthew 13:54—
Jesus went to his
hometown and
taught the people
in the synagogue
in a way that
amazed them.
People were
asking, "Where did
this man get this
wisdom and the
power to do these
miracles?"*

*J*esus amazed people everywhere he went. They saw God in him but couldn't quite be sure they recognized what they saw. Jesus' hometown recognized God's wisdom and power but, because they had seen Jesus grow up from a little boy, they doubted their own sense of knowing. God's power is power that heals. God's wisdom is wisdom that produces kindness and love. And Jesus lived them both. What a shame that God was there and so few knew.

A Moment with God

Ask God to help you recognize his power and wisdom today.

*For Further Reading:
Matthew 13:54–14:34*

257

The Local Lost and Found

*Matthew 18:12—
What do you
think? Suppose a
man has 100
sheep and one of
them strays. Won't
he leave the 99
sheep in the hills
to look for the one
that has strayed?*

A Moment with God

Thank God that he
never gives up on
you. His limitless
love will rescue you
from any plight.

*For Further Reading:
Matthew 18:12-14*

*T*he ewe spied a section of grass that looked somewhat greener than where the shepherd was leading. She meant to come right back, but her thick wool became entangled in the thorns and trapped her. She was lost and alone. Darkness arrived. She heard the howl of hungry wolves nearby. Fear and hopelessness gripped her. Then, suddenly, the great shepherd appeared, gently untangled her, picked her up, put her on his strong shoulders, and carried her back to the herd. Have you wandered away from God? Do you feel lost? Alone? Afraid? Hopeless? He longs to have you back, and he's searching for you. He loves you so much.

Impossible!

*Matthew 19:26—
Jesus looked at
them and said, "It
is impossible for
people ͵to save
themselves ͵ but
everything is
possible for God."*

*T*he road to hell is paved with
assumptions. The disciples
disclosed a very common theory
that Jesus destroyed with his
statement. Because they thought
rich people receive special
treatment from God, they were
shocked when Jesus spoke of
the difficulties the rich encounter on their way into the kingdom of God.

The real question isn't "Can
God make a person's salvation
possible?" but rather "Why
would God want to make a
person's salvation possible?" The
Bible's answer is grace. By his
life, death, and resurrection,
Jesus threaded the impossible
needle on our behalf. Why would
we want to remain in an impossible situation when our escape
has been made possible?

A Moment with God

Picture as vividly as
you can what Jesus
did to save you, and
then thank him for
that gift.

*For Further Reading:
Matthew 19:16-30*

259

The Relentless Tenderness of God

*Matthew 23:37—
Jerusalem,
Jerusalem, you kill
the prophets and
stone to death
those sent to you!
How often I
wanted to gather
your children
together the way a
hen gathers her
chicks under her
wings! But you
were not willing!*

A Moment with God

Thank God that,
even in your greatest
need, even when
you resist his
tenderness, still
he seeks you.

*For Further Reading:
Matthew 23:29-39*

*T*he great measure of the love of
God is seen by his response to
those who turn from him. Judas
betrayed Jesus, yet, at the very
moment of betrayal, Christ called
him friend. And it was six weeks
after Peter's denial of Christ that
he was most greatly used by God.
God loved us when we were still
his enemies. Christ came to *seek*
those who were lost. Jesus did
have harsh words of warning for
those who resisted the ways of
God, yet even then there was
tenderness. He wept over the
wayward and spoke of his desire
to gather and shelter them, as a
hen does her young.

The Unsolvable Mystery

*Matthew 24:30, 36—
Then the sign of the
Son of Man will
appear in the sky. .
. . "No one knows
when that day or
hour will come.
Even the angels in
heaven and the Son
don't know. Only
the Father knows."*

*H*ave you ever heard people predict when the Lord will return and the events of the end times will unfold? For many Christians, deciphering the events of the end times is a favorite pastime. Despite the best efforts of Christians, the mystery of the end times is one that won't be solved until the events actually occur. The reason is simple: God has chosen not to reveal that information to us. We can comfort ourselves with the fact that God has revealed everything we need to know about our future, namely, how we can have eternal life in his presence. Because of God's revelation, we can rest assured that our future is secure.

A Moment with God

Thank God for the fact that he has revealed everything you need to know concerning the end times.

*For Further Reading:
Matthew 24:1-51*

Divine Values

*Matthew 26:10—
Since Jesus knew
what was going
on, he said to
them, "Why are
you bothering this
woman? She has
done a beautiful
thing for me."*

A Moment with God

Thank God for
accepting you as
you are.

*For Further Reading:
Matthew 26:6-13*

*I*f you sometimes feel insignificant, remember this story of this scorned woman. When everyone else rejected her actions, Jesus honored her for her demonstration of faithfulness. While everyone else was whispering critical words, Jesus welcomed her presence. Why? Because God is a judge of hearts, not appearances. God has compassion for even the loneliest of hearts. God peels away the layers of sin, of failure, of rejection, and he sees only the penitent, the earnest, the lovely. Do you wonder what God thinks of you? Replace that wonder with confidence: God values your heart.

Good for What Ails You

SEPTEMBER 20

Mark 2:17—
When Jesus heard
that, he said to
them, "Healthy
people don't need a
doctor; those who
are sick do. I've
come to call sinners,
not people who
think they have
God's approval."

*B*oil down all reasons why people reject God, and you find the heart of their problem: They don't think they need him. They self-assuredly deem themselves healthy by their own merits and so are unable to accept him—or anything besides themselves—as lord over their lives. But to those who know they have nowhere else to turn, no matter how far down society's ladder they may be, God is willing to reach out and touch them with his hope of salvation. His purpose in this world is to redeem lost humanity to himself, no matter where he has to go to find them.

A Moment with God

Think about people you know who don't know the Lord. Be one of the ways God reaches out to them.

For Further Reading:
Mark 2:1-17

The Weather Man

Mark 4:39—
Then he got up,
ordered the wind
to stop, and said to
the sea, "Be still,
absolutely still!"
The wind stopped
blowing, and the
sea became
very calm.

A Moment with God

Visualize our whole world resting in God's hands. Praise God for his infinite power and his attention to the needs of this world.

For Further Reading:
Mark 4:35-41

Who has the power to stop an oncoming hurricane? Imagine the disciples' reaction when Jesus stood up in a violent storm and commanded the wind to stop—and it did. Was it a coincidence: He speaks and the wind stops? During the next few weeks when they saw Jesus heal the sick, multiply food from a small lunch, and walk on the water, they began to understand that this man did what only God can do. As Jesus demonstrated, God's power is unlimited. What is impossible for people is easy for God. That limitless power was never used frivolously. The disciples watched Jesus unleash his power to help needy people and build the faith of the disciples. Jesus wanted everyone watching to know they can trust God in any situation.

Stand Up and Be Counted!

Mark 8:38— If people are ashamed of me and what I say in this unfaithful and sinful generation, the Son of Man will be ashamed of those people when he comes with the holy angels in his Father's glory.

*I*t matters to God that his children own up to their relationship with him. It is not enough to love him in heart and mind but never admit it. God demands allegiance. He requires devotion. To him religion is certainly *not* a private matter. It is, in fact, very public. God recognizes that his ways and his words do not fit comfortably in any generation. But it is not comfort he demands. It is obedience, faithfulness, and pride in following him. God will not recognize in public those who do not do the same for him.

A Moment with God
Ask God to give you the strength to stand up for him today.

For Further Reading: Mark 8:31-38

Jesus Values Children

*Mark 10:16—
Jesus put his arms
around the
children and
blessed them by
placing his hands
on them.*

A Moment with God

Thank God for his tender love for children. Ask him to help you show that same love to the children you know.

*For Further Reading:
Mark 10:13-31*

*I*sn't this a tender picture? Jesus gathers the children into his arms and blesses them. Unlike his disciples, who thought Jesus had better things to do with his time than fuss with children, Jesus values children. He values their unquestioning love, their innocent trust, and their unfettered joy. Jesus told the people around him that they needed to be like children if they wanted to be part of his kingdom. This picture reminds us that no human being is too young, too small, or too messy to deserve God's full attention and love.

Very Little Becomes Very Much

Mark 12:43b-44– This poor widow has given more than all the others. All of them have given what they could spare. But she, in her poverty, has given everything she had to live on.

What can we possibly do that an infinite God would appreciatively notice? How could we ever merit commendation from a praiseworthy and perfect God? What could prompt God to think of us gratefully and honor us openly? The answer is different from what we might expect. Jesus complained of those who made a great show of their generosity, who gave large sums of money amid great fanfare, in order to be noticed and applauded. In contrast, he singled out a poor woman who gave so little that the gift scarcely had any monetary value whatsoever. She had little to give, yet she gave it all. He never misses such quiet generosity and unassuming service.

A Moment with God

Remember: God is appreciative and attentive to your service, your kindness, your generosity.

For Further Reading: Mark 12:35-44

Ever After

Mark 13:31—
The earth and the
heavens will
disappear, but my
words will never
disappear.

A Moment with God

Beyond all that is physical in this world, his word remains forever true and forever there. Praise him for being able to hold eternity in his hands.

For Further Reading:
Mark 13:24-37

*F*orever is deeply planted in the human heart. We yearn for it, this deep sense of "ever after." We want our stories to end with it, our accomplishments to ring of it, and our own souls to be safe in it. It is part of what pulls us to God and his word, this yearning for an endless tomorrow.

These words of Jesus stand as a seal of guarantee that today, this moment, we can hold something eternal in our hands: Something that will never change. . . . and will go on and on and on, something that will stand, no matter what the time or the place or the culture. His word draws us to him and forever points us in the right direction.

Turning Point

SEPTEMBER 26

*Mark 14:36—
He said, "Abba!
Father! You can
do anything. Take
this cup ⌊of
suffering⌋ away
from me. But let
your will be done
rather than mine."*

*F*or a moment, in the garden of
Gethsemane, eternity hung on a
prayer. Jesus was honest with
the Father. Knowing what he
would soon face, Jesus ex-
pressed his heartfelt wish that
there could be some other way.
He acknowledged his identity
with God and God's power. In his
humanity he requested a way out.
But he firmly remained committed to doing God's will, even if
that meant the "cup of suffering."

The Bible tells us Jesus often
prayed. This verse allows us to
listen in as Jesus prayed. If Jesus
had rejected the cup of suffering,
it would have reverted to its
rightful owners (us). Jesus
considered that option in prayer,
but he remained true to his
character as our savior.

A Moment with God

Identify some area
of your life which
you have seldom
discussed with the
Lord. Make that the
focus of prayer
today.

*For Further Reading:
Mark 14:32-42*

Favored by the Lord

*Luke 1:27-28—
The angel went to
a virgin promised
in marriage to a
descendant of
David named
Joseph. The
virgin's name was
Mary. When the
angel entered her
home, he greeted
her and said, "You
are favored by the
Lord!"*

A Moment with God

Praise God for the
fact that he can and
does use anyone to
accomplish his will.
Consider how you
can make yourself
available to be used
by the Lord.

*For Further Reading:
Luke 1:1-80*

*I*t is easy for us to place the so-called heroes of the faith on a pedestal. The tendency is to assume that God chose the worthiest, godliest, and most deserving people to carry out his purposes, almost as though the famous characters of Scripture earned the right to be used of God. The truth is that God favors people by using them in extraordinary ways. He does not choose people according to a merit system. He used Mary to accomplish his perfect will; he can also use you to perfect his plan.

Freed from Sin

*Luke 5:20—
When Jesus saw
their faith, he
said, "Sir, your
sins are forgiven."*

A sin of which we haven't let go is like a paralysis: It hardens our hearts, diminishes our tenderness, and literally stiffens us, making us resistant to God's voice. Sin keeps us from running into the arms of our Father. We're spiritually paralyzed and frozen. Perpetual sin is insidious and powerful; without our realizing it, sin takes over, pushing us farther from God. But God is able to forgive us. When we accept forgiveness, we are like the paralyzed man in this story: Energized by forgiveness, our life begins again.

A Moment with God
Think about a sin that comes between you and God. Ask for his forgiveness.

*For Further Reading:
Luke 5:17-26*

If Only I Could . . .

*Luke 8:43-44—
A woman who had
been suffering from
chronic bleeding for
twelve years was in
the crowd. No one
could cure her. She
came up behind
Jesus, touched the
edge of his clothes,
and her bleeding
stopped at once.*

A Moment with God

God always has time
for you. Praise him
that he cares
enough about you to
be available.

*For Further Reading:
Luke 8:40-48*

Twelve years of suffering. The doctors offered her no hope. Then, with nowhere left to turn, she heard about Jesus. She heard he could help her, but she didn't want to impose. So she quietly snuck up behind him, thinking, "If only I could touch the edge of his clothes. . . ." She did, and she was healed instantly. In spite of the crowd, Jesus had time for her. Sometimes you may feel that God doesn't have time for you. Your prayers don't seem to get past the ceiling. God seems distant and uncaring. If only you could touch him. You can. He knows you are there. He is available.

He Knows the Future

Would you want to know the details of your future? Could you handle knowing when and how you are going die? Jesus knew his future. Being fully God, he possessed total prior knowledge of his betrayal and tortuous death. When he tried to explain these future events to his disciples, they didn't understand.

God knows everything past, present, and future. We may struggle to comprehend how God can know what's ahead for us, but we can be confident that God has a plan for our life. God doesn't want us to be anxious about our future. He knows what is ahead and promises to give us every-thing we need when we face the challenging moments of life.

SEPTEMBER 30

Luke 9:44-45—
"Listen carefully to what I say. The Son of Man will be betrayed and handed over to people." They didn't know what he meant. The meaning was hidden from them so that they didn't understand it.

A Moment with God

Praise God for his greatness that allows him to know the past, present, and future. Thank God that he uses his knowledge to guide your life.

For Further Reading: Luke 9:43-62

The God Who Gives

Luke 11:9—
So I tell you to
ask, and you will
receive. Search,
and you will find.
Knock, and the
door will be
opened for you.

A Moment with God

It is God's nature to give. Generosity drives him. Kindness motivates him. What do you need from God today?

For Further Reading:
Luke 11:1-13

*H*ow generous is God? How predictable is his kindness? He is like a consistent and sensitive father. If you ask him something, he will answer. If you knock, the door will open. If you seek, you will find. This is the nature of God. He meets our asking, our knocking, our seeking with answers, open doors, and satisfying discoveries. Think of a father. It is a father's heart to give . . . and to give with kindness and generosity. Jesus taught us that only a sadistic father would answer his child's request for food with something that would disappoint or endanger her. Our heavenly Father loves us enough to give only the best.

Ultimate Power

*Luke 12:5—
I'll show you the
one you should be
afraid of. Be afraid
of the one who has
the power to throw
you into hell after
killing you. I'm
warning you to be
afraid of him.*

Our turn of the century society tends to take God lightly. While we become excited about technology break throughs and medical advances, we hardly remember God. Even though it was God who gave us the technology to create microchips and the knowledge to research DNA, we forget about him.

Jesus reminds us, though, that our God is real and powerful. He's the one we should be impressed by.

You'll enjoy the benefits of technology today: you'll probably brew a pot of coffee, microwave a lunch, turn on your computer, and get behind the wheel of your car. Each time you take advantage of technology, try to remember that God is far greater than any gadget that makes our lives convenient.

A Moment with God

Ask God to help you focus on the big picture today, not the details.

*For Further Reading:
Luke 12:1-12*

275

Come On Home

*Luke 13:34—
Jerusalem,
Jerusalem, you kill
the prophets and
stone to death
those sent to you!
How often I
wanted to gather
your children
together the way a
hen gathers her
chicks under her
wings! But you
were not willing!*

A Moment with God

Thank God for never
giving up on you.
Come on home.

*For Further Reading:
Luke 13:22-35*

A mother drifts in and out of
sleep—and prayer—agonizing
over her son, hoping the next
thing she hears is his key in the
lock, not another middle-of-the-
night phone call from the police
station or the emergency room.
How can the little boy she
nursed as a baby, nurtured
through childhood, and sacrificed her life for care so little?
Sometimes she feels like shak-
ing him. But more often, she
weeps and wishes she could
hold him close, feel his head
resting against her shoulder,
hear him say how much he loves
her. One more time. That's the
kind of love God has.

Found!

*F*aced with a crowd of the curious and questioning, Jesus told stories. He taught about God while he talked about people. The shepherd's love for a single sheep, the woman's joy over a lost coin found, and the father's welcome of a lost son all speak of God's overwhelming love.

In the third story, the father's love sees past rejection, rebellion, waste, and foolishness to embrace the wayward son. His experience illustrates a humbling truth for all of us: We are never closer to God's forgiveness than at the moment when we consider our sins unforgivable. We don't surrender to God on our terms. We surrender without any conditions. God's love receives his children again in a heartbeat.

OCTOBER 4

Luke 15:31-32—His father said to him, "My child, you're always with me. Everything I have is yours. But we have something to celebrate, something to be happy about. This brother of yours was dead but has come back to life."

A Moment with God

Have you told God recently how wonderful it is to be part of his family?

For Further Reading: Luke 15:11-32

The Little Mustard Seed That Could

*Luke 17:5-6—
"If you have faith
the size of a
mustard seed, you
could say to this
mulberry tree,
'Pull yourself up by
the roots, and
plant yourself in
the sea!' and it
would obey you.*

A Moment with God

Consider ways in
which your faith
might be put to use.
Thank God for the
fact that he works
through your faith to
accomplish great
things.

*For Further Reading:
Luke 17:1-37*

Jesus taught his followers that they had responsibilities toward God. First and foremost, they had a responsibility to have faith in him. When the disciples asked for more faith, Jesus replied that even the smallest amount of faith was enough to accomplish miracles. Christians today still have a responsibility of faith in God. God works through the faith of his people, empowering us to accomplish tasks and face situations beyond any of our expectations. Do you have faith the size of a mustard seed? If so, what might God's empowerment allow you to do?

Only in Christ

*Luke 20:17—
Then Jesus looked
straight at them
and asked, "What,
then, does this
Scripture verse
mean: 'The stone
that the builders
rejected has
become the
cornerstone'?"*

*L*ove me, love my son, says God.
Reject my son, reject me, says
God. The warning echoes
throughout Scripture: No one
comes to the Father except
through the son. Religious
leaders, attempting to dilute
Jesus' growing popularity, were
exposed by Jesus' teaching.
They understood the message
but, even so, considered moving
up their timetable to arrest Jesus
at this point. Only their fear of
the people restrained their
deadly plot. They did not
comprehend the route to God—
only through Christ, the cornerstone of heaven.

A Moment with God

Spend a moment
with God, express-
ing your love of his
son and your
gratitude for
Christ's sacrifice.

*For Further Reading:
Luke 20:1-19*

Anguished Prayer

Luke 22:42—
Father, if it is your
will, take this cup
⌊*of suffering*⌋*away*
from me.

On the verge of the most difficult experience of his life on earth—suffering crucifixion for our sins—Jesus prayed in anguish to his Father. He knew he needed to empty himself of his own will and submit completely to his Father's will, even though that would bring him much pain. Jesus gave us a powerful model here. As we face life's excruciating experiences, we too must pray, emptying ourselves of our own will and asking God to reveal his will to us. We must trust God to strengthen us for the task of doing his will.

A Moment with God

Submit yourself and your will to God in fervent prayer. Then trust him to strengthen you.

For Further Reading:
Luke 22:39-46

Dying with Jesus

OCTOBER 8

*Luke 23:42-43—
Then he said,
"Jesus, remember
me when you enter
your kingdom."
Jesus said to him,
"I can guarantee
this truth: Today
you will be with
me in paradise."*

*I*t is one thing to say, "Jesus died for the sins of the world." It is quite another to say, "Jesus died for me." How great is the selflessness of his death in our place? Put yourself into the scene. Visualize yourself also there on that hillside in agony as death too slowly approaches. You know the pain he feels; you feel it also. It astounds you to think, even at the extreme of human pain, he summons all his energy to pay attention to you. Even in this extreme of unimaginable suffering, it is not himself for whom he suffers. It is for you.

A Moment with God

Can you hear Christ's words as if spoken to *you*, "You will be with me in paradise"?

For Further Reading: Luke 23:1-49

Alive!

Luke 24:5—
The women were
terrified and bowed
to the ground. The
men asked the
women, "Why are
you looking among
the dead for the
living one?"

A Moment with God

Spending too much time in graveyards lately? Ask the living God to point you toward the living and fill you up with his abundant life.

For Further Reading:
Luke 24:1-12

We spend so much of our lives looking in the wrong places for fulfillment. While searching for contentment, we often forget to look to Christ. We try to adopt habits of successful people, and we imitate the actions of those we admire. We look to everyone—except Christ.

The problem is, most of what this world has to offer won't last through eternity. As a result, we spend most of our time searching for happiness in a world that doesn't have eternal happiness to offer. It's like trying to find happiness while walking through a graveyard.

Rather than look around the world for your fulfillment, look to Christ—the one who can show you the meaning of abundant life.

Who Has Seen God?

OCTOBER 10

John 1:17-18— The Teachings were given through Moses, but kindness and truth came into existence through Jesus Christ. No one has ever seen God. God's only Son, the one who is closest to the Father's heart, has made him known.

What would *Time* magazine pay for a picture of God? We're not suggesting something mystical like sun rays bursting through a cloud but a clear, focused picture of the actual creator and ruler of this universe.

In early history, people saw God as a pillar of fire or knew him as the giver of commands through prophets and leaders like Moses. But God wanted people to see him more clearly as a God of kindness and truth. So God the Father sent Jesus the Son into the world with a human body—the clearest possible picture of God. It's vitally important to know what Jesus said and what he did during his life here on earth because Jesus was God in a human body teaching us and helping us know the God we cannot see.

A Moment with God

If you want a clear picture of God, look at Jesus Christ. He is fully God in a human body.

For Further Reading: John 1:1-18

Communicating Love

John 3:16—
God loved the
world this way: He
gave his only Son
so that everyone
who believes in
him will not die
but will have
eternal life.

A Moment with God

Thank God for his love—not the feeling of it, but the reality of it.

For Further Reading:
John 3:1-21

God showed his love with an ultimate sacrifice. God showed his love with the loss of something dear. God showed his love with pain and suffering. God showed his love with a cross and a grave and a thorny crown and a dark sky. God showed his love by doing what he knew had to be done in order for his followers to be forgiven and complete. God showed his love through cries of forsakenness and tears of betrayal. God showed his love in a raging passion, a thunderous proclamation. And God has never stopped showing it.

Cross Your Eyes

*H*ave you seen those pictures that when you look at them normally, you see nothing in particular? But if you look *through* the flat picture, or cross your eyes, a full three-dimensional image will pop out at you. God is like that. When you look through human eyes at the physical world, you don't see anything unusual. But if you look beyond the world through the cross of Jesus, you will see God. God is beyond the physical world. He is spirit. And if we choose to let him into our lives, he adds a new dimension. He takes flat lives and makes them full.

OCTOBER 12

John 4:23—Indeed, the time is coming, and it is now here, when the true worshipers will worship the Father in spirit and truth. The Father is looking for people like that to worship him.

A Moment with God

Praise God that he is above and beyond this physical world. Thank him for his Spirit, who lives in you.

For Further Reading: John 4:1-42

Bread

John 6:35—
Jesus told them, "I am the bread of life. Whoever comes to me will never become hungry, and whoever believes in me will never become thirsty."

A Moment with God

In what ways has Jesus been the bread of life in your life? Have you told him that recently?

For Further Reading: John 6:22-40

*J*esus repeatedly said the unexpected. The truth turned out to be the most outrageous expressions anyone had ever heard. Jesus' "I am" statements were particularly shocking. Everyone knew what he meant. He was claiming to be God. Most of those who heard him refused to look at the facts. They refused to believe he was God.

Jesus had already changed water to wine, multiplied loaves and fishes, and stilled the sea. But rather than put their faith in him, they hoped he would set up some social reforms. If Jesus was king, the people thought, no one would go hungry again. But Jesus didn't come to start a bread line. He came to open a bread-of-life line. He came to identify those who would come and believe.

To God Be the Glory

John 7:18—
Those who speak
their own thoughts
are looking for
their own glory.
But the man who
wants to bring
glory to the one
who sent him is a
true teacher and
doesn't have
dishonest motives.

*H*ow can you tell when someone is lying to you? What do you look for—a twitching eye, a stammer, perhaps light beads of sweat above the person's lip? How can you tell when someone is teaching false principles concerning God? Jesus provided some guidelines for answering this question when the Pharisees accused him of being a false teacher. In short, Jesus explained that if a teaching gives glory to the teacher, it is false; if it gives glory to God, it is true. God's truth is capable of transforming lives and changing the world. Christians are responsible for discerning between his truth—that which brings glory to him—and false teaching.

A Moment with God

Praise God for the power of his truth. Ask him for guidance in recognizing it.

For Further Reading:
John 7:1-53

287

Jesus Wept

OCTOBER 15

*John 11:33—
When Jesus saw
her crying, and the
Jews who were
crying with her, he
was deeply moved
and troubled.*

A Moment with God

When heartache comes and sorrow chokes you, can you visualize the tears of Christ as he feels with you?

*For Further Reading:
John 11:1-44*

Jesus was summoned to the deathbed of a friend but arrived late—beyond the point of death and beyond the burial. Jesus did not seem to arrive in a swirl of hope, quieting fear and reversing disease. Wasn't it too late for healing? Hadn't the time for miracles come and gone? The family grieved. The drama that followed illustrated more than Christ's authority over natural laws and death, it also illustrated the depth of his compassion. Jesus wept. These were not casual tears. This was grief so strong that bystanders were amazed at the depth of his emotion. "See how much Jesus loved him." The astounding thing is that he feels such deep emotion for us amid all our concerns.

The Holy Helper

John 14:16—
I will ask the
Father, and he
will give you
another helper
who will be with
you forever.

*J*esus knew the disciples would feel like abandoned children when his time on earth was complete. He could foresee their loneliness. He could anticipate their sadness. He knew they would be fearful and worried, so he announced his last gift to them: the Holy Spirit, a holy helper who would reside in the hearts of believers. What was his purpose in sending this "holy helper"? To give peace to God's children, to help them when they are troubled, to guide them when they are confused about God's will in their lives. In other words, the "Holy Spirit" is the guide to peace.

A Moment with God

Talk to the "holy helper" about your life. Seek his counsel today. Listen for his answers.

For Further Reading:
John 14:1-28

289

The Root of Your Strength

John 15:5—
I am the vine. You
are the branches.
Those who live in
me while I live in
them will produce
a lot of fruit.
But you can't
produce anything
without me.

A Moment with God

Before you run
yourself ragged
doing all that you
can, plug into his
word, and let
his power
rejuvenate you.

For Further Reading:
John 15:1-27

God created humans with a body and a mind to do many things. The human brain itself is simply unfathomable, remaining a wonder even to those who invest their lives studying it. But as smart as we can become, as far as we can push the boundaries of our endurance, God has placed this limit on us: We can't do anything of lasting value without him. The best we can do ourselves is nothing compared to what he can do through us. He has created us to run on his power alone, and even the weakest who do this can become the mightiest of all.

No One Left Standing

*John 18:6—
When Jesus told
them, "I am he,"
the crowd backed
away and fell to
the ground.*

How many armed soldiers does it take to arrest a traveling preacher with no history of violence? The Jewish leaders had a troop of soldiers with them when they tried to apprehend Jesus. They never suspected that a short sentence from this man's mouth could have knocked them off their feet.

While sitting on the ground, some of those men may have felt the awesome power that resided in Christ's human body. During the next twenty-four hours Jesus willingly restrained his power, allowing these men to arrest, beat, and crucify him. Jesus could have stopped his execution by speaking just one word. Instead he followed God's eternal plan and laid down his life as payment for our sins.

A Moment with God

Imagine how you will respond when you stand in the presence of God and see his glory and power. Bow down and worship him today as you will on that glorious day in the future.

*For Further Reading:
John 18:1-40*

291

What Is Salvation?

John 20:31—
But these miracles
have been written
so that you will
believe that Jesus
is the Messiah, the
Son of God, and so
that you will have
life by believing in
him.

A Moment with God

Thank God today for your salvation experience.

For Further Reading:
John 20:24-31

*U*Ultimately God saves us from death and gives us life. He chooses to give second chances. He chooses to go to great lengths to forgive and to teach us to do the same. God is a God of salvation. He is a rescuer. Through Jesus' miracles he showed this over and over again. He showed us that he sees our plight. And while he does not fix it all, he provides a way to rise above it eventually. He sees our futures if left to ourselves, and he saves us to a better one.

Powerful Witness

When God took Jesus to be with him once again in heaven, he did not abandon his people. Instead he sent his Spirit, who would live in the hearts of the men and women who believe in him. This Spirit would give power to share the story of who Jesus is with people all over the world. When we see God at work in our lives and share that insight with a friend, God's Spirit is active. When we make a Bible available to a person who does not know about the Lord, God's Spirit is at work. Watch today for God's Spirit to work through you.

OCTOBER 20

Acts 1:8—
But you will receive power when the Holy Spirit comes to you. Then you will be my witnesses to testify about me in Jerusalem, throughout Judea and Samaria, and to the ends of the earth.

A Moment with God

Reflect on ways God's Spirit has allowed you to tell about his love with other people. Praise him for his power.

For Further Reading: Acts 1:1-14

Backbone

OCTOBER 21

*Acts 5:29—
Peter and the
other apostles
answered, "We
must obey God
rather than
people."*

A Moment with God

Ask God to help you spot moments of compromise today and to reinforce your backbone of convictions.

*For Further Reading:
Acts 5:17-42*

*T*he disciples had been warned not to mention Jesus' name in public. They respectfully disobeyed. Their response established a precedent for all believers—cooperation with the authorities unless ordered to disobey or disregard Jesus.

Given the nature of the world, following Jesus will involve difficult choices. The pressure may not come from the same source Peter faced. But sooner or later we will have to make costly choices in order to maintain integrity. God expects ultimate obedience. Those who firmly practice that principle find every other decision clearer. Christians who demonstrate spiritual backbone will encourage many others toward faithfulness.

The Great Escape

Think of Peter's great escape. We are struck by the drama of it: The impossibly bleak circumstances, the startling intervention, the happy ending, the power God displayed. But aren't we also struck by the mystery of God's purpose? Acts 7 recounts the execution of Stephen. There was no intervention for him, yet he was not loved by God any less. God has a loving purpose for us as well, and nothing will thwart it. Armed guards and human authorities cannot frustrate the plan of God, neither can death. Sooner or later, we will stand, and the chains will break and fall away, powerless to hold us.

OCTOBER 22

*Acts 12:7—
Suddenly, an
angel from the
Lord stood near
Peter, and his cell
was filled with
light. The angel
nudged Peter's
side, woke him up,
and said, "Hurry!
Get up!" At that
moment the chains
fell from Peter's
hands.*

A Moment with God

It is just as important to ask God to reveal his purpose as it is to thank him for his care.

For Further Reading: Acts 12:1-18

God's Witnesses

*Acts 14:15b-17—
The living God
made the sky, the
land, the sea, and
everything in
them. In the past
God allowed all
people to live as
they pleased. Yet,
by doing good, he
has given evidence
of his existence.*

A Moment with God

Take a moment
today to consider
some piece of God's
creation—a tree or a
mountain or a sea.
Imagine and wonder
at the God big
enough to have
created it.

*For Further Reading:
Acts 13:48–14:18*

*T*his rock upon which we live,
hurtling through space, stands
as evidence of the existence of
God. To the people of Paul's day,
the thought that all that surrounded them was somehow
some huge mistake, some
unchoreographed coincidence,
would have been completely
preposterous. Created things
pointed with authority to the
certainty of a creator. Of that
they needed no convincing. The
question in their hearts was not
"if" or "how"; the question was
"who." Paul simply filled in the
blank, and those "prepared for
everlasting life believed."

Everyday Miracles

Would you say that it is easier or more difficult to be a Christian today than it was in the first-century church? If you could witness firsthand the kind of miracles that the apostles and early Christians witnessed, how do you think it would affect your faith? For that matter, why doesn't God seem to give concrete evidence of his miraculous power anymore? The answer, of course, is that God's power is still evident everywhere. Every day, people recover from life-threatening illnesses, escape from potential disasters, and experience dramatic life changes—all as a result of God's power.

OCTOBER 24

Acts 16:25-26—Around midnight Paul and Silas were praying and singing hymns. . . . Suddenly, a violent earthquake shook the foundations of the jail. All the doors immediately flew open, and all the prisoners' chains came loose.

A Moment with God

Consider the evidences of God's power that you've seen in just the past few weeks. Praise him for the power that he displays to you every day.

For Further Reading: Acts 16:1-40

Heavenly Legacy

Acts 20:32—
I am now entrust-
ing you to God and
to his message that
tells how kind he is.
That message can
help you grow and
can give you the
inheritance that is
shared by all of
God's holy people.

A Moment with God

Compare your earthly legacy with your heavenly inheritance. Have you thanked God lately for what you expect to receive?

For Further Reading:
Acts 20:32-38

Have you ever received an inheritance? Do you expect to be the recipient of an inheritance someday? Your inheritance may be, by earthly standards, great wealth—money, stocks, land. But perhaps you're anticipating the opposite: your parents owned little, so you inherit little. Then there are those who expect to inherit nothing from their parents. Some of us will inherit no material goods or wealth from those who've gone before. Yet all of us are all recipients of an inheritance that cannot be measured: the salvation of our souls!

God's Nightstand

Acts 23:11—
The Lord stood
near Paul the next
night and said to
him, "Don't lose
your courage!
You've told the
truth about me in
Jerusalem. Now
you must tell the
truth about me in
Rome."

Sarah keeps a Bible on her nightstand. She sleeps alone in a rough neighborhood, and if she hears gunfire or other noises in the night, she turns on a small lamp and begins to read. God stands beside her in the night, offering his presence as comfort. God did the same for Paul two thousand years ago. He does the same for you. He stands beside you no matter how dark the times may seem. Are you lonely? He is there beside you. Are you afraid? He stands to protect you. Have you failed him? He is still there, holding you and accepting your confession. The light of his presence shines through the darkest night.

A Moment with God

Thank God that he is always with you, no matter where you are or what the circumstances, offering you comfort.

For Further Reading:
Acts 22:30–23:11

God's Finger- prints

Romans 1:19-20— What can be known about God is clear to them because he has made it clear to them. From the creation of the world, God's invisible qualities, his eternal power and divine nature, have been clearly observed.

A Moment with God

Thank God today for making a fabulous and complex world for you to enjoy. Most of all, thank God for revealing himself to you.

For Further Reading: Romans 1:1—2:13

New discoveries in forensic science are helping police solve crimes where no eyewitness is available. The presence of a single hair or a flake of skin can reveal a DNA profile that can be matched to a suspect to solve the mystery.

Some people still think the origins and purpose of our world is a mystery. But God's finger-prints are all over the "scene of the crime." If you look closely, you will see reliable evidence that God exists and is the designer and creator of this earth.

God left countless clues because he didn't want anyone to miss the opportunity of knowing the truth and worshiping the one, true God. Through the Holy Spirit, God makes himself known to everyone.

The Rewards of Faith

OCTOBER 28

Romans 3:22— Everyone who believes has God's approval through faith in Jesus Christ. There is no difference between people.

God delights in the heart of faith. He is not looking for riches or sacrifice. He does not long for performance or achievement. What he looks for are hearts that believe in him even when they do not see him. What he approves of are people who do not claim to be self-made. God looks for the simple faith that draws people to prayer. God applauds the firm belief that he is there, and he cares.

A Moment with God

Thank God that he is with you everywhere you go. Ask God to help you remember that he is present with you throughout the day.

For Further Reading: Romans 3:21–4:3

Invincible Love

OCTOBER 29

Romans 8:38—
I am convinced
that nothing can
ever separate us
from God's love
which Christ Jesus
our Lord shows us.

A Moment with God

How can you express
your gratitude for the
changeless love of
God? What response
does it prompt
within you?

For Further Reading:
Romans 8:1-39

*T*hink of all that might thwart
God's love. What might stand
between us and the love of a
friend? Death separates us, of
course, but so can the pressures
and circumstances of life. Stress
can wear on us, put us on edge,
erode our well-being and clear
thinking. Troubles can make us
seem like we are no longer the
people we once were. We
disappoint one another because
people, plagued by shortcomings, are not yet perfect in the
art of love. Hardship and human
foibles can come between loved
ones who now feel estranged by
circumstance. In contrast, God
loves us with an everlasting,
unchanging, invincible love.

Get Out of Jail Free

*Romans 11:32—
God has placed all
people into the
prison of their own
disobedience so that
he could be merciful
to all people.*

We have a condition only God can heal: our inborn resistance to him. He created us with a freedom to choose, and we have all chosen our own way. As a result, we deserve his wrath, his justice, and his swift, severe, and eternal punishment. Yet the judge of all the earth exercises his freedom to visit us with his mercy, to enter the prison our sins have caged around us, to come down to death row, where we sit without hope, and to extend a pardon only a fool would resist. His justice is great, but his mercy is greater.

A Moment with God

Thank God that he has come to you in your sins and offered you the gift of mercy and forgiveness.

*For Further Reading:
Romans 11:25-36*

True Fulfillment

Romans 12:1—
Brothers and
sisters, . . . I
encourage you to
offer your bodies as
living sacrifices,
dedicated to God
and pleasing to
him. This kind of
worship is
appropriate
for you.

A Moment with God

Lord, don't allow me to slip, slide, slink, or slither off the altar I'm living on today.

For Further Reading:
Romans 12:1-21

Have you ever counted the ways people search for meaning in life? Some people try to find fulfillment through money, promotions, hobbies, marriage, sex, children, or retirement. In themselves, each of these fails to bring us the fulfillment we're looking for because they are not the ultimate purpose for which God created us.

Paul gave us the answer that we're looking for. What's the best for us? What will bring us ultimate fulfillment? To be a living sacrifice to God. We were created to honor God and give him glory. If we spend the rest of our lives praising him, we'll find the fulfillment we're looking for.

Wise Fools

Human beings have used their God-given wisdom and intelligence to accomplish some remarkable things. The invention of the automobile, the exploration of space, and the development of computer technology are a few examples. However, when human intelligence is directed against God and his truth, our wisdom becomes folly and nonsense. God's perfect plan of salvation is the epitome of simplicity. Yet it cannot be appreciated by human brilliance. God, in his perfect wisdom, created a plan of salvation that can only be received in a person's heart.

NOVEMBER 1

1 Corinthians 1:18—
The message about the cross is nonsense to those who are being destroyed, but it is God's power to us who are being saved.

A Moment with God

Praise God for his unfathomable wisdom. Remember to call on that wisdom as you face the decisions and challenges of everyday life.

For Further Reading:
1 Corinthians 1:10-31

Temple of God

NOVEMBER 2

*1 Corinthians 6:19—
Don't you know that
your body is a
temple that belongs
to the Holy Spirit?
The Holy Spirit,
whom you received
from God, lives in
you. You don't
belong to yourselves.*

The apostle Paul's admonition stands firm even today: Our earthly bodies have the unique assignment of providing a residence for the Holy Spirit. Our bodies do not belong to us. They are temples that house the Holy Spirit of God. Would the God of heaven and earth choose to live in a temple desecrated by filth and sin? That's Paul's point. When our bodies engage in sins of the flesh, we are making God an unwilling participant.

A Moment with God

Ask God to help you make your body a temple for his Holy Spirit. Banish from your "temple" anything that doesn't belong there.

*For Further Reading:
1 Corinthians 6:12-20*

Marital Fidelity

1 Corinthians 7:2—But in order to avoid sexual sins, each man should have his own wife, and each woman should have her own husband.

God values the marriage relationship. In his wisdom he ordained that a husband and wife should be sexually faithful to each other, avoiding all situations that would threaten their marital oneness. A husband's or wife's commitment to his or her spouse says, "I have chosen you to be my spouse, and I promise to be faithful to you—emotionally, mentally, physically, and spiritually—no matter what." God's wisdom for married couples mirrors his relationship to us. He will stand by us faithfully, caring for us as a faithful husband cares for his wife.

A Moment with God

Praise God for his wisdom for marriage relationships and for his faithfulness to you.

For Further Reading:
1 Corinthians 1:1-23

*1 Corinthians 8:6—
But for us, "There is
only one God, the
Father. Everything
came from him,
and we live for him.
There is only one
Lord, Jesus Christ.
Everything came
into being through
him, and we live
because of him."*

A Moment with God

Praise God for his
excellent greatness
and his singular
lordship over
this world.

*For Further Reading:
1 Corinthians 8:1-13*

One Way . . . and Only One Way

The popular opinion of our modern society is shifting toward accepting all religions and concepts of God as equally valid. It is now politically correct to let people construct and worship their own deities.

Unfortunately, the basis of such religious tolerance is without merit. The Bible clearly states that there is only one God and only one Lord—Jesus Christ. That narrow truth is hard for some people to accept in our increasingly pluralistic culture.

Our world wasn't put together by a committee of gods. The world was the masterpiece of one designer and creator. The one, true, living God is the original cause behind our world and our lives.

Learning to Love

When we think of God giving gifts to people, we naturally think of the gifts of health or success, clothing, food, or forgiveness. But of all his gifts, few equal the beauty of his gift that enables *us* to give. In God, we discover a new capacity to give and receive love. In him, we find the ability to understand love in a higher, unselfish form. In Christ, we learn to love as he loved. His love is marked by patience, kindness, and self-sacrifice. It is remarkable enough to be loved by God in such a way. It is truly astonishing that he would teach us to express such love to others.

1 Corinthians 13:6-7—
[Love] isn't happy when injustice is done, but it is happy with the truth. Love never stops being patient, never stops believing, never stops hoping, never gives up.

A Moment with God

Think of how God expresses his love to you. How can you more closely emulate that love this week?

For Further Reading:
1 Corinthians 13:1-13

Victorious!

*1 Corinthians
15:55—
Death, where is
your victory?
Death, where is
your sting?*

A Moment with God

The power of God defeated death. The word is in the past tense. Is there any battle raging in your life right now that requires more power than that?

*For Further Reading:
1 Corinthians 15:1-58*

*E*ver get stung by a bee? The pain just keeps on coming. As the injected poison slowly seeps cell by cell, an area 100 times the size of where the stinger penetrated is eventually affected. Even though the sting itself took place hours before, the tissue can remain swollen, painful, and inflamed for days. The damage goes on and on. It is much the same with the venom of sin in our lives. But there's good news! A powerful cure exists that neutralizes that venom, repairs the damage, and actually heals. Victory is ours, achieved through the power of Jesus Christ and his resurrection. Stingless, defeated death can cause no more pain.

Does He Care Enough to Comfort?

*I*t might seem that a God of might and strength, of holiness and righteousness would have little time for such a simple thing as comforting a human heart, however broken it might be. But God does take the time to comfort. It could appear that a God so incomprehensible, so large, and so powerful would have little interest in healing a wounded soul, however pained it might be. But God does have the interest. Through his Son he has known suffering, and from his suffering he comforts us. The God of comfort cares infinitely and comforts the same way.

NOVEMBER 7

2 Corinthians 1:4—He comforts us whenever we suffer. That is why whenever other people suffer, we are able to comfort them by using the same comfort we have received from God.

A Moment with God

Talk to God today about your distresses, and let him comfort you.

For Further Reading:
2 Corinthians 1:3-7

Isn't It Ready Yet?

*2 Corinthians 6:2—
God says, "At the
right time I heard
you. On the day of
salvation I helped
you." Listen, now is
God's acceptable
time! Now is the
day of salvation!*

A Moment with God

God's timing is
always perfect.
Thank God that he
hears your prayers
and answers them
according to his
schedule.

*For Further Reading:
2 Corinthians 5:11–6:2*

Shari rushed through the door. "Is dinner ready?" Her mom kept stirring and replied, "You'll have to wait just a few minutes." Shari sat and talked with her mother for awhile. Finally, she asked again, "Isn't it ready yet?" Her mother replied, "Yes. It was just about done when you came in. But I let it cook a little longer so you would take the time to visit with me before you ate and left again." God's timing is sometimes like that. We pray and plead for an answer, but God wants to give us more than the answer. He wants to give us himself. He sometimes waits so that we will spend more time with him.

Poverty

*2 Corinthians 8:9—
You know about the
kindness of our
Lord Jesus Christ.
He was rich, yet for
your sake he
became poor in
order to make you
rich through his
poverty.*

Jesus demonstrated the most costly form of kindness. He switched places with us. We tend to think of kindness as a gift from our surplus. We are kind to someone and go on our way, unchanged. But Jesus completely took on our spiritual poverty and shared his spiritual riches with us.

Jesus emptied himself (see Philippians 2:7) so that he could literally become "our kind." Thus he made us "rich" by becoming our kind of teacher, our kind of savior, and our kind of Lord. Our kindness must have more of the sacrificial character Jesus demonstrated. Kindness meets a real need.

A Moment with God

Ask the Lord for an opportunity to demonstrate true kindness to someone before this day is over.

*For Further Reading:
2 Corinthians 8:1-9*

313

Strength in Weakness

*2 Corinthians
12:7b—
Therefore, to keep
me from becoming
conceited, I am
forced to deal with a
recurring problem.
That problem,
Satan's messenger,
torments me to keep
me from being
conceited.*

A Moment with God

Consider a weakness
or affliction of yours
that you've asked
God to remove.
Ask the Lord to
demonstrate his
strength in your
weakness.

*For Further Reading:
2 Corinthians 12:1-21*

*I*f someone asked you to sum up the key principles of the Christian life in one sentence, how would you respond? Here's one suggestion: Consider what society tells you to do to get ahead—and then do the exact opposite. Think about the "contrary" nature of Christ's teachings. Want to be honored? Be a servant. Want to be first? Be last. Want to be strong? Be weak. Paul had a difficult problem (he doesn't specify what it was) that he asked God three times to remove. In response, God pointed out that his power is strongest when we are weak. When we stop relying on our own efforts and turn everything over to God's power, we allow ourselves to become instruments of his will.

314

He Judges Hearts

NOVEMBER 11

*Galatians 2:16—
Yet, we know that
people don't
receive God's
approval because
of their own efforts
to live according
to a set of stan-
dards, but only by
believing in Jesus
Christ.*

What a heavenly relief! God judges hearts, not actions. What a joyful revelation! God asks for belief, not deeds. Throw out the checklists, toss out the rule books, pack up the laws. God's acceptance won't come to us like a gold star on a report card. God's approval isn't won by passing tests. God doesn't police his people; he accepts those who accept him. The answer is faith in Christ, says Paul. If anyone should understand this, it's Paul, the ultimate policeman. But he gave up his "badge" for simple belief. What a clear reminder of what God does for his children.

A Moment with God

Meditate on the great gift of acceptance through Christ. Express your gratitude through prayer and praise.

*For Further Reading:
Galatians 2:15-21*

An Inheritance from God

NOVEMBER 12

*Galatians 4:5—
God sent him to
pay for the freedom
of those who were
controlled by these
laws so that we
would be adopted
as his children.*

A Moment with God

Think about the
implications. You are
more than forgiven.
You are part of the
family of God.

*For Further Reading:
Galatians 3:24—4:7*

*T*he couple sat in the judge's
chamber, a four-year-old boy
seated on a chair between them,
his face barely rising above the
table ledge. Solemnly, but
pleasantly, the judge explained
the adoption, stressing that the
young boy was now the couple's
"heir-at-law." He now had every
family right, just as certainly as if
he had entered the family
through birth rather than
adoption. This, of course, is what
God has done for us. It is a
measure of his love and grace
that he does so much more than
merely offering forgiveness. He
also stands waiting, with the
eagerness of all adoptive parents,
to make us part of his family. We
become heirs-at-law.

Fruit of God

NOVEMBER 13

*Galatians 5:22—
But the spiritual
nature produces
love, joy, peace,
patience, kindness,
goodness, faithful-
ness, gentleness,
and self-control.*

*I*magine your shock if you found
a pineapple and a coconut
growing on an apple tree. You'd
be stunned because it's not
supposed to happen. You expect
apples to grow on apple trees.
That's the way nature works.

When we receive the Holy
Spirit, we begin to grow spiritual
fruit. The Spirit makes this
spiritual fruit natural to us.

Where did Paul get this list
of fruit we're to have? Each of
these attributes is a characteristic of God. Paul gave us this list
because as Christians we're to
imitate God. Just as children
often pick up character traits
from their parents, Christians are
to pick up traits of their heavenly
Father.

A Moment with God

Which characteristic
in today's verse is
missing in your life?
Ask God to help you
imitate him in this
area.

*For Further Reading:
Galatians 5:1-23*

The Giver's Best Gift

NOVEMBER 14

Ephesians 2:8-9—
God saved you
through faith as an
act of kindness. You
had nothing to do
with it. Being saved
is a gift from God.
It's not the result of
anything you've
done, so no one can
brag about it.

A Moment with God

Try to comprehend what it means for God to love you unconditionally—just as you are. Thank God today for accepting you and loving you even when your behavior is far from perfect.

For Further Reading:
Ephesians 2:1-10

Some people still don't understand God. They explain their relationship with God by describing how often they go to church or how moral they are compared to others. They think winning God's favor and going to heaven are directly related to their good behavior. From a human view it seems fair, but God's way of dealing with us has nothing to do with our good behavior.

God loves us so completely that his salvation is offered to everyone as a free gift. In his kindness and mercy he forgives even the worst sinner who puts his faith in Jesus Christ. The full price of our forgiveness has been paid in full by the death of his son, Jesus, on the cross.

The One and Only

NOVEMBER 15

*Ephesians 4:16—
He makes the
whole body fit
together and unites
it through the
support of every
joint. As each and
every part does its
job, he makes the
body grow so that it
builds itself up
in love.*

There is one God, not many. He is the center of the church's worship and the church's service. He is the unifying factor. He establishes his church around one goal and asks for its singleheartedness. In following God, his people do not become more distinct, more segregated. God is not the God of division or individuality. He is the God of oneness and harmony. He is the binding force for a broken world, the adhesive for a struggling church, and the unifying factor for lives that are falling apart.

A Moment with God

Ask God to show you the broken places in your life and relationships.

*For Further Reading:
Ephesians 4:1-16*

319

Rejoicing in Difficulty

*Philippians 1:27—
Live as citizens
who reflect the
Good News about
Christ.*

*R*oad rage and credit card fraud.
Irate customers and unreasonable bosses. We can be taken
advantage of in countless ways.
What is the best response when
we're blind-sided by someone
who causes us trouble? We
should follow the instructions of
this verse by representing Christ
wherever we go.

No matter what happens to
us, we remain God's ambassa-
dors, and we are to represent
him and treat others with the
same kindness and patience he's
given to us.

A Moment with God

Think about the next
twenty-four hours.
Ask God to help you
represent him well
through any
unexpected
circumstances.

*For Further Reading:
Philippians 1:1-31*

Developing an Attitude

Philippians 2:5—Have the same attitude that Christ Jesus had.

We are invited to imitate Christ's attitude, even though we will never have to start from the same altitude. Jesus had to give up more, travel farther, and go deeper into life than will ever be required of us.

Jesus emptied himself of godly rights. We must empty ourselves of pride. Jesus' service was beyond measure. We do well not to measure ours either but to give ourselves in service. Someone said it well: Serve until it hurts. Someone else said it better: Serve until there are no more opportunities to serve.

Jesus came as Savior to serve everyone at all times in all places. We get to imitate him where we are. That's a large enough order for a lifetime.

A Moment with God

Lord, teach me to serve with an attitude—Christ's.

For Further Reading: Philippians 2:1-11

Bridging the Grand Canyon

*Philippians 3:9b—
I didn't receive
God's approval by
obeying his laws.
The opposite is
true! I have God's
approval through
faith in Christ.*

A Moment with God

Thank God for the fact that you, as a sinner, are able to have a relationship with the Holy Lord.

*For Further Reading:
Philippians 3:1-21*

Y

ou've probably heard many analogies to illustrate the impossibility of reconciling with God through good works: It's like trying to bridge the Grand Canyon with a yardstick; it's like trying to reach the moon by standing on a stepladder. God is holy, which means that he is separated from sin. No amount of good works can earn God's approval. Because God is holy, the only way we, as sinners, can hope to have a relationship with him is through faith in his Son. While obeying God's laws is vital to maintaining a close relationship with God, faith is the only way to establish the relationship.

A Calm Amid the Storm

*T*he storm came up suddenly on the lake that night, as storms often do there, even to this day. The boat rose and fell on waves that seemed certain to overwhelm it. Through it all—through the fierceness of the wind and the fury of the sea—Jesus slept. When finally awakened, it didn't take much to calm the story. A quiet command, and nature obeyed. The raging storm was followed by a supernatural peace. The peace that followed the storm was the same kind of peace that Christ experienced *during the storm*, as he slept through the noise and drama, trusting his Father. It is just such a peace that the apostle Paul described, the kind that God promises will follow our faith.

NOVEMBER 19

Philippians 4:6-7— Never worry about anything. But in every situation let God know what you need in prayers and requests while giving thanks. Then God's peace, . . . will guard your thoughts and emotions through Christ Jesus.

A Moment with God

People may find a certain serenity through relaxation techniques and optimistic thoughts. God's peace goes beyond this, holding the promise of a supernatural calm.

For Further Reading: Philippians 4:1-23

The Power Source

*Colossians 1:11—
We ask him to
strengthen you by
his glorious might
with all the power
you need to
patiently endure
everything with joy.*

A Moment with God

His glorious might strengthens us. Ask for that strength today in a situation you cannot handle on your own.

*For Further Reading:
Colossians 1:1-12*

*E*ver experience a power failure? Isn't it impressive how fast everything becomes useless? The most powerful machinery and impressive tools in the world just occupy space when the connection to the power source is interrupted. We are much the same. Sometimes we are tempted to try to run on some "alternative fuels" (like our past experiences, strengths, and expertise). But we soon find that we don't seem to run very far or very long on them. Besides that, these "alternatives" aren't very renewable. The power we need comes from only one source. It comes with a guarantee of no worries or interruptions of service. His power is glorious because it is completely reliable, always available, and in plentiful supply.

324

Hearts That Sing

*Colossians 3:16—
Let Christ's word
with all its wisdom
and richness live in
you. Use psalms,
hymns, and
spiritual songs to
teach and instruct
yourselves about
⌊God's⌋kindness.
Sing to God in
your hearts.*

*F*ocusing on things that are above enriches our daily walk. Hearts that belong to Christ are hearts that sing, regardless of circumstance, regardless of position, regardless of what is going on in our lives. Modeling the qualities that we see in God, we his "holy people," want to exhibit the attributes of God: kindness, humility, gentleness, patience. All of these are traits that God's followers can strive to attain, traits that bring the follower nearer to the heart of God. And where God lives, wisdom and richness abide. The practices mentioned in this verse (psalms, hymns, spiritual songs) remind us that expressing our praise helps us understand God better.

A Moment with God
Sing to God in your hearts! Give thanks to the Lord for his many kindnesses.

For Further Reading: Colossians 3:1-17

Just What You Need

NOVEMBER 22

1 Thessalonians 1:4—
Brothers and sisters, we never forget this because we know that God loves you and has chosen you.

A Moment with God

Reflect on God's love for you. Trust him to show you his love by providing just what you need.

For Further Reading: 1 Thessalonians 1:1-10

*T*he orphanage was running low on food. They desperately needed bread and milk. They had no money and nowhere to turn, so they prayed. Almost immediately, a bread truck and milk truck each had minor problems that stranded them near the orphanage. Since the cargo would have spoiled anyway while waiting on help, each driver donated the contents of his truck to the orphanage. God loved the orphans and provided for them. God loves us, and he will give us good will, mercy, and peace when we need them. We may sometimes feel helpless with nowhere to turn, but God in his endless love will always provide just what we need.

Conqueror of Death

*1 Thessalonians
4:14—
We believe that
Jesus died and
came back to life.
We also believe
that, through
Jesus, God will
bring back those
who have died.
They will come
back with Jesus.*

*A*ll religions sound helpful and nice until you face life's greatest challenge—death. Mohammed, Buddha, Confucius, and the rest gave us clever sayings about death, but none of them escaped its lethal grip. It's hard to have much hope about eternal life when the religion's founder could do no better than die like all the rest of us.

Jesus stands apart from all other religious figures because of his resurrection from the grave. God's mighty power conquered death and brought Jesus back to life. For that reason alone Christians can find comfort and hope in the promises of God when death comes knocking. God is God because he has the power to do what it is impossible for people to do.

A Moment with God

Think about the mighty power of God that gives each believer eternal life. Thank God for providing eternal life to all who trust in Jesus Christ.

*For Further Reading:
1 Thessalonians
4:1-18*

Might for Right

*2 Thessalonians
1:11—
With this in mind,
we always pray
that our God will
make you worthy
of his call. We also
pray that through
⌊his⌋ power he will
help you accom-
plish every good
desire.*

A Moment with God

Ask God to help you
see his power in
your life today.

*For Further Reading:
2 Thessalonians
2:13-16*

*I*t is a miracle that a God so
powerful, so strong, so able, so
mighty would not use his power
against a sinful people but rather
use it to benefit us. It is God's
power that helps the widow face
her new loneliness. It is God's
power that gives a wounded
spouse the strength to forgive.
It is God's power that moves a
broken person to try again.
It is God's power that enlivens
weakened and static lives and
makes them strong and dynamic.
It is God's power that saves,
releases, frees, and refreshes.
Might that could so easily
destroy, because of his kindness,
empowers.

Blessed Assurance

NOVEMBER 25

*2 Thessalonians
3:16—
May the Lord of
peace give you his
peace at all times
and in every way.
The Lord be with
all of you.*

*O*f all the things God provides, perhaps the one that meets us on the deepest level of human need is his peace. We can pray for healing, we can ask for a miracle, we can believe him for the impossible, but we also can trust that he is masterminding all the time. This gives us confidence to take "no" for an answer because he gives us his peace and his assurance. We are comforted because he is aware of everything in our lives and is working them together for our good. We have security that, no matter what he allows us to face, he will give us the reserves to endure it. With him, we have the ability to look death in the eye and give God the glory. His peace gives us the power to persevere.

A Moment with God

God can calm your troubled soul and lift your heavy heart with just one word.

*For Further Reading:
2 Thessalonians
3:1-18*

Kings Do As They Please

*1 Timothy 1:16—
Good will, mercy,
and peace from
God the Father
and Christ Jesus
our Lord are
yours!*

A Moment with God

Paul perceived himself as on a mission for the king of heaven. God *is* king. What is his "mission" for you?

*For Further Reading:
1 Timothy 1:1-11*

*I*n a country without a king, and in which even our elected officials are routinely ridiculed and sometimes disregarded, it is difficult to understand the idea of a "monarchy." In fact, in this country, even the presidency has been emptied of much of its mystique and awe. We are suspicious of elected officials, and there is so much competition between the branches of government, it may sometimes seem a wonder that anything productive is even achieved. In a true monarchy, the word of one person is final and authoritative. The king speaks, and his word is law. God is a monarch. He can do whatever he pleases. The wonder is, it pleases him to be generous and gracious.

Doxology

*1 Timothy 1:17—
Worship and glory
belong forever to
the eternal king,
the immortal,
invisible, and only
God. Amen.*

What thoughts usually prepare you for worship? What character trait of God most quickens your heartbeat? Which of God's attributes inspires awe in you? Paul shared a special list with Timothy in this verse. For Paul, God deserved worship. It belonged to him and no one else.

We worship God for his majesty and supreme royalty. God is also the ageless one, unchanging and tireless. His invisibility heightens his immensity: he would have to reduce himself in order for us to see him. And God is the only God.

Although we bear God's image, we are also so unlike him that humility in his presence should always be our aim.

A Moment with God

Let me never lose my amazement as a creature, Lord, that I'm allowed the privilege of knowing, loving, and worshiping my creator.

*For Further Reading:
1 Timothy 1:12-17*

Misplaced Trust

NOVEMBER 28

*1 Timothy 6:17—
Tell those who have
the riches of this
world not to be
arrogant and not
to place their
confidence in
anything as
uncertain as
riches. Instead, they
should place their
confidence in God.*

A Moment with God

First Timothy 6:17
tells us that God
"richly provides us
with everything to
enjoy." Thank him
for the abundance of
his blessings.

*For Further Reading:
1 Timothy 6:1-21*

*P*eople who draw a relatively large salary are said to make a "comfortable" living, as though money and comfort are synonymous. While most people pay lip service to the maxim, "Money can't buy happiness," the pursuit of wealth remains one of our society's favorite pastimes. What is it about wealth that inspires confidence in those who possess it? We're all aware of the negative side of riches—greed, paranoia, arrogance, and so on. The riches that God offers, however, have no such consequences. No matter how much money a person accumulates, the wealth is temporary. In contrast, the riches that God provides are sufficient to sustain us for eternity.

The Source of Our Strength

2 Timothy 1:9b-10—
Before the world began, God planned that Christ Jesus would show us God's kindness. Now with the coming of our Savior Christ Jesus, he has revealed it. Christ has destroyed death.

*I*t's interesting to note the use of the themes "death" and "kindness" in the same passage. At first glance, the two wouldn't seem to be related to one another. We usually don't use death and kindness in the same thought, do we? Yet, in the history of the world, what greater kindness has ever been demonstrated than the death of Christ and his power to defeat death? That's why the writer claims Christ's kindness as the source of strength because God's kindness was exhibited in his powerful destruction of death. Now death is powerless to the Christian. And only God's kindness remains.

A Moment with God

Think about God's power and kindness. How has he been kind to you?

For Further Reading: 2 Timothy 1:1—2:26

The Best Instruction

NOVEMBER 30

2 Timothy 3:16—
Every Scripture
passage is inspired
by God. All of them
are useful for
teaching, pointing
out errors,
correcting people,
and training them
for a life that has
God's approval.

A Moment with God

Ask God to reveal more and more of himself to you as you study his word.

For Further Reading:
2 Timothy 3:1-16

*I*n our quest for knowledge, education, and learning, let's not forget the best source of instruction: God's word. We can count on the Bible to be authoritative, true, and practical. In it God not only shows us that we are creatures made in his image but also that he wants us to be in personal relationship to him. God's word show us how to live and what he has done to make up for the times we live selfishly or wrongly. And in his word, God shares with us the greatest news of all: That if we believe that he has died for our sins, we will live with him forever.

The Example of Love

DECEMBER 1

*Titus 1:2b-3—
God, who never
lies, promised this
eternal life before
the world began.
God has revealed
this in every era by
spreading his word.*

God has an answer for all skeptics. For those who want to see something before they believe it, God has put on an impressive display. God's love isn't the hype of an advertising blitz or the promises of a political campaign. He sent his own son, Jesus, into our troubled world to live among us and set us free from being slaves to our own selfish desires. God didn't just tell us to love others. He modeled it for us by sending Jesus into the world.

God doesn't beat us up with condemnation or scold us with harsh words. He shows us how satisfying and beneficial it is to serve others. Jesus' life is a model for those who want to make something significant out of their own.

A Moment with God

When God gives a command to you he also sets an example for you. Thank God for giving all the skeptics of this world a clear picture of genuine love.

*For Further Reading:
Titus 1:1-16*

Short on Kindness?

*Titus 2:11-12—
After all, God's
saving kindness
has appeared for
the benefit of all
people. It trains us
to avoid ungodly
lives filled with
worldly desires so
that we can live
self-controlled,
moral, and godly
lives in this
present world.*

A Moment with God

Take a deep breath, talk with God as the trusted, kind friend who he is.

*For Further Reading:
Titus 2:1-15*

God is not a list of do's and don'ts. He is not an angry landlord snooping around to find fault. He is not a super-sized hall monitor who does his job best when he brings down punishment on someone's head. God is, ultimately, benevolent and kind. God wants and knows what is best. He gives guidelines that act as a map to achieve that "best." God cares for the sparrows and tends to minute details. He creates beauty and walks in a path called salvation. He is trustworthy in his kindness and will not suddenly turn into a raging, unrecognizable fury. Because he is kind and also wise, we can trust him.

Before and After

*H*e was angry, hateful, verbally abusive. In time, his wife became fearful, took the children, and went into hiding. If you met him today and heard such a description, your jaw would drop in disbelief. The change has been that complete. He is now so soft-spoken and kind, his wife speaks of him as having been "gentled" by God. And who could argue, really? Such dramatic change is rarely achieved through our own effort. Paul said the kindness and love of God has appeared and has brought with it the prospect of astonishing change. People who knew you before you met God may drop their jaw in disbelief.

DECEMBER 3

Titus 3:3—
We were mean and jealous. We were hated, and we hated each other. However, when God our Savior made his kindness and love for humanity appear, he saved us, but not because of anything we had done to gain his approval.

A Moment with God

Not all of the changes God brings about are instantaneous. What work remains to be done in you?

For Further Reading:
Titus 3:1-15

A Gift Already Given

*Philemon 1:3—
Good will and
peace from God
our Father and
the Lord Jesus
Christ are yours!*

A Moment with God

Where in your life do you really need the fullness of God's peace today?
Thank him for this indescribable gift.

*For Further Reading:
Philemon 1:1-22*

Never mistake the peace of God as the absence of conflict. That may be a definition we are willing to settle for when talking about peace between nations or neighbors. But it is an answer that misses the point entirely when talking about the peace of God. The peace of God can exist right smack dab in the middle of conflict; in fact, it thrives there.

Peace is a wondrous gift waiting to be unwrapped and enjoyed. It is full and tangible and, best of all, as Paul reminds Philemon, is already his.
And yours.

Jesus Knows

*Hebrews 2:18—
Because Jesus
experienced
temptation when
he suffered, he is
able to help others
when they are
tempted.*

You face temptations every day—desires that beg you to submit to evil. You know better, but sometimes the desire becomes so strong that you assume the only way to get rid of the desire is to fulfill it. Jesus demonstrates a better solution. During his life he faced many temptations that you face—desires for fame, fortune, power, sensual pleasures. Those desires caused *suffering*, according to the Bible. Yet Jesus never gave in. Now, when we suffer in our temptation, we have a God who understands and offers to help us through it. He can help you fight the desires when they come.

A Moment with God

Thank God that he understands your suffering during temptation. Pray for his help the next time you face temptation.

For Further Reading: Hebrews 2:11-18

339

A Spiritual Scalpel

Hebrews 4:12a— God's word is living and active. It is sharper than any two-edged sword and cuts as deep as the place where soul and spirit meet, the place where joints and marrow meet.

A Moment with God

Having heard your word, Lord, help me be a faithful doer of it.

For Further Reading: Hebrews 4:1-12a

*T*he modern equivalent of the word *sword* might be *laser*. It wounds in order to heal. It cuts through red tape, red herrings, and all the barriers of the human mind and heart (see Jeremiah 17:9-10). God's word confronts (judges) us. It demonstrates that God knows us inside out.

You can probably recall numerous times this year when God's word has confronted your life. Your responses have determined much of your walk with God. The more God's word has gotten *in* your mind, the more you've found it to be *on* your mind.

The Living Word

Hebrews 4:12b-13—God's word judges a person's thoughts and intentions. No creature can hide from God. Everything is uncovered and exposed for him to see. We must answer to him.

*H*ave you ever read a book or poem, viewed a piece of art, listened to music, or watched a film that touched you deeply? The word of God can have a similar effect. God's word, like a sword, penetrates to your innermost being. There it judges your thoughts and attitudes. The inner life of a Christian is often a strange mixture of genuinely spiritual motivation and motivation based on human wants. Only the omniscience of God and his word can distinguish between the two. Because God is omniscient, nothing is hidden from his sight.

A Moment with God

Consider the penetrating effect of God's word. Ask the Lord to help you discern the motivations behind your everyday actions and attitudes.

For Further Reading: Hebrews 4:12b-16

Forgive and Forget

*Hebrews 10:16-17—
"This is the promise
. . . 'I will put my
teachings in their
hearts and write
them in their
minds.' " Then he
adds, "I will no
longer hold their
sins and their
disobedience
against them."*

A Moment with God

Spend some quiet
time with God,
discussing past
secrets. Deal with
private issues,
thanking him for the
gift of forgiveness.

*For Further Reading:
Hebrews 10:15-23*

Someone's listening. Someone's watching. All of our thoughts, all of our actions are observed by someone—not just any someone, but the one true God. How does it feel to realize that we have no secrets? Does it bring a smile, a sense of relief and hope? Or does it make us squirm and flush with embarrassment? If we constantly remind ourselves that God is always on-line, will we alter our thoughts? Does an awareness of God's presence in our lives motivate us to act and speak in a manner that is pleasing to God? How does it feel to realize the promise of Hebrews? God, the great forgiver, who knows our secret sins, forgives those sins. What a blessed promise!

One Thing's for Sure

*Hebrews 11:10—
Abraham was
waiting for the
city that God had
designed and
built, the city
with permanent
foundations.*

You can put your faith in a home
alarm system, only to enjoy the
shrill, unexpected reminders of
computer malfunctions. You can
put your faith in a 10% raise, only
to see the roof start leaking and
hear the dentist prescribe new
braces. There is simply nothing in
this world that can give a true
100% guarantee. Except God. He
will be here after loved ones die,
after health deteriorates, after the
temporary pleasures of sin have
become prisons of guilt and
shame. He will be here when
everything else you've known
has melted away.

A Moment with God

End your friendship
with things that are
destined to perish,
and stake your claim
with the God of
eternity.

*For Further Reading:
Hebrews 11:1-40*

A Perfect Law

*James 1:25—
However, the
person who
continues to study
God's perfect
teachings that
make people free
and who remains
committed to them
will be blessed.*

A Moment with God

God's agenda for you
is that you become
all he planned for
you to be. Ask him to
rekindle that
yearning in you.

*For Further Reading:
James 1:1-27*

*F*ew people are truly satisfied with
what they have so far become.
When we are honest with ourselves, we can identify shortcomings that are enough to make us
discontent, yearning to be better.
But how are we to change? We
could notice our faults and
become swamped with discouragement. We could see ourselves
for what we are and quickly deny
those imperfections—like a
person who looks in a mirror, then
turns away, quickly forgetting
what he looks like. In contrast,
when we focus intently on God's
Word and purpose to obey it, we
will find that very Word has the
power to transform us.

God's VIPs

DECEMBER 11

*James 2:5—
Listen, my dear
brothers and
sisters! Didn't God
choose poor people
in the world to
become rich in
faith and to
receive the
kingdom that he
promised to those
who love him?*

*M*oney! Money! Money! The best things in life cost money—or do they? God doesn't think that wealth is the ticket to happiness or eternal life. God warns us not let money become a substitute in our life for him. God resists people who are filled with pride (perhaps from being wealthy).

People with money don't get more of God's attention. He is more interested in people who grow strong in faith because they possess less wealth. In God's sight it is wrong to give preferential treatment to rich people. God commands us to look at people the way he does and value a poor person's faith more than a rich person's bank account.

A Moment with God

Thank God for his compassion for the poor and the struggling. Praise him for valuing people for their faith rather than their riches.

*For Further Reading:
James 2:1-13*

Let There Be Peace

James 3:18—
A harvest that has
God's approval
comes from the
peace planted by
peacemakers.

A Moment with God

Ask God to show you the way to peaceful-ness today within your own soul.

For Further Reading:
James 3:13—4:10

*B*ecause God is the creator of the universe, the Lord of everything, his approval should be sought and valued. So it is important to know exactly of what God approves. He approves of lives lived with his own peaceful nature. His approval shines each time an agenda is put aside so that his love can prevail. God approves of a harvest of peace. He is the seed that bears it, the rain that pours down on it, and the sun-shine that breathes life into it.

Good Suffering

*1 Peter 1:7—
The purpose of
these troubles is to
test your faith as
fire tests how
genuine gold is.
Your faith is more
precious than gold,
and by passing the
test, it gives praise,
glory, and honor
to God.*

Contemporary society says, "Pain is bad. Avoid it at all costs." But if we are realistic, we admit that as long as we live in this fallen world, we will suffer painful experiences. Scripture tells us that suffering can be good because God can use our suffering to test us, to shape our faith, and to purify us. God doesn't leave us alone to face our problems; he walks with us through them. When we come through the problems, our faith not only remains intact but also is strengthened. God turns our suffering into a purer faith.

A Moment with God

Give your painful experiences to God, asking him to use your suffering to shape your faith.

*For Further Reading:
1 Peter 1:1-9*

347

Hear Here

*1 Peter 3:12—
The Lord's eyes are
on those who do
what he approves.
His ears hear their
prayer. The Lord
confronts those
who do evil.*

A Moment with God

Thank God that your good deeds and prayers do not go unnoticed. You always have his undivided attention.

*For Further Reading:
I Peter 3:8-22*

*H*ave you watched the movie *It's a Wonderful Life* this year? You probably know the story. George Bailey is unselfish and does good all of his life. He faces, however, an unexpected crisis that causes him to believe that God has not been attentive to his ways. He begs for God to be attentive to his prayer.

Sometimes it seems as if your good deeds and prayers go unnoticed, while others around you who break the law and take unethical shortcuts get all the breaks. God really is watching, though. His eyes see your life and his ears hear your prayers. He is listening and watching.

Restoration, Strength, and Support

*T*rue or false: Becoming a Christian means that you will never have to face suffering. Most Christians would probably respond to this statement with an emphatic, heartfelt "False!" Christians are no strangers to suffering. God never promised a problem-free existence for his people. What he does promise is that suffering will not defeat his people. God, in his kindness, vows to restore the suffering Christian, to provide his strength and support when it is needed most. Fortunately, the kindness of God is infinitely more powerful than any suffering you'll ever face.

DECEMBER 15

1 Peter 5:10—God, who shows you his kindness and who has called you through Christ Jesus to his eternal glory, will restore you, strengthen you, make you strong, and support you as you suffer for a little while.

A Moment with God

Consider some examples of kindness that God has shown you in the past few weeks. Thank him for restoring you, strengthening you, and supporting you.

For Further Reading: 1 Peter 5:1-14

Honest to God

DECEMBER 16

*2 Peter 1:5—
Because of this,
make every effort
to add integrity to
your faith; and to
integrity add
knowledge.*

A Moment with God

Ask God to help you make integrity a priority in your dealings with others today.

*For Further Reading:
2 Peter 1:3-15*

*P*eter preaching on the topic of honesty? Peter, the apostle who denied Jesus three times, admonishing us to be people of integrity? Can you think of a better advocate for honesty than one who has failed the test? Peter knew the torment of being dishonest. If anyone ever learned from a mistake, it's this apostle. In fact, he puts integrity at the top of the list when naming the fruits of the spirit. Why? Look at verse three: God has called us by his own glory and *integrity*. If we want to be like God, we will strive to be people of integrity.

God Judges Evildoers

*2 Peter 2:9—
Since the Lord did
all this, he knows
how to rescue godly
people when they
are tested. He also
knows how to hold
immoral people for
punishment on the
day of judgment.*

*D*o you ever feel overwhelmed by the immorality in today's world? Do you feel helpless to stand against the leaders of the immorality? Just as God protected Lot, a godly man of Old Testament times, from the disgusting sexual immorality of the city in which he lived, God will protect us from the evils of our present world. Not only has God promised to help us stay pure in the midst of immoral influences, but he has also promised to punish the evildoers who perpetuate the immorality. We can take heart because God is in control.

A Moment with God

Praise God for his protection. Trust him to judge and punish people who perpetuate evil.

*For Further Reading:
2 Peter 2:1-10*

351

Time Is Only Temporary

*2 Peter 3:8—
Dear friends, don't
ignore this fact: One
day with the Lord is
like a thousand
years, and a
thousand years are
like one day.*

**A Moment
with God**

Since God knows so
much more about
time than you do,
spend more time
today getting to
know him.

*For Further Reading:
2 Peter 3:1-18*

The first Christians wondered if Jesus would come back during their lifetime. They began to wonder if Christ's promised return was really true. To make matters worse, skeptics mocked them saying, "So, where is this Jesus after all?"

Although people were doubting and mocking God, Peter reminded Christians that God remains trustworthy. The problem is that our sense of time is immediate. We think about today, tomorrow, and next week. But God's sense of time is eternal. He can look at a thousand years in one hand and a single day in the other and not see any difference.

You can have confidence about your future and Christ's return. God has everything under control.

You Can Count on It

*1 John 1:9—
God is faithful
and reliable. If we
confess our sins, he
forgives them and
cleanses us from
everything we've
done wrong.*

Can we count on God to forgive our sins? God made an enormous investment in our world for just that purpose when he sent his son, Jesus, to die on the cross. What happened on the cross provides a bottomless account of forgiveness for all who confess their sins. God is fully capable of forgiving our sins. That's his business.

God's previous history regarding forgiveness reveals there is no limit to his mercy, whether we are first time or repeat offenders.

A Moment with God

Praise God for his never-ending mercy to you. Give thanks that there is nothing you need to hide when you pray to him.

*For Further Reading:
1 John 1:1-2:2*

What Is God?

DECEMBER 20

*1 John 4:8—
The person who
doesn't love doesn't
know God, because
God is love.*

*T*he bottom line is this. God is the very essence of love. God doesn't just show love. He doesn't just feel love. He doesn't just require love. God *is* love. He was love in the creation of the world. He was love in the Bethlehem manger. He was love on the cross and in the resurrection. And he is love today. The person who doesn't love, doesn't know him. Because to know God is to know love.

A Moment with God

Give God full control of your decisions today so that his love will shine through the hustle and bustle.

*For Further Reading:
1 John 4:1-19*

Praying Confidently

DECEMBER 21

*1 John 5:14—
We are confident
that God listens to
us if we ask for
anything that has
his approval.*

When we pray, we often approach God timidly, unsure that he will hear us. We subconsciously wonder if God listens only to important people or to important requests. However, we don't need to be shy. God wants to hear all our prayers. He tells us to come confidently to him. He assures us that, if we ask him for things that he knows are good for us, he will say yes. Just as parents want to give good things to their children, God our heavenly Father wants to give us good experiences, relationships, and joys.

A Moment with God

Confidently pray to your Father, pouring out your needs to him. Be confident that he will give you whatever is good.

*For Further Reading:
1 John 5:1-21*

Candles, Stars, and Wishing

DECEMBER 22

*2 John 1:3—
Good will, mercy,
and peace will be
with us. They come
from God the
Father and from
Jesus Christ, who
in truth and love is
the Father's Son.*

A Moment with God

Thank God for his wondrous generosity. Reflect on his blessings in your life today and praise him.

*For Further Reading:
2 John 1:1-13*

*M*ake a wish before you blow out the candles. Wish upon a star. Toss a few coins into the wishing well. What do you wish for when you have the chance? You probably wish for a good life, peace, and true happiness. Candles, stars, and wishing wells cannot grant your wishes, but the God of heaven can. He freely gives his blessings to you everyday: a beautiful sunset, the blossoming flower, the sparkle in the eye of a loved one. He is so generous with his gifts. Before you even ask, he gives. Every blessing comes from the hand of God.

Steady As He Goes

Jude 1:24—
God can guard you
so that you don't
fall and so that you
can be full of joy as
you stand in his
glorious presence
without fault.

She was half-scared, half-frus-
trated. She wanted to learn to
ride, but that out-of-control feeling
was overwhelming. That hard,
black pavement looked like a
knee scrape waiting to happen.
But her father just tightened his
grip on the back of her bike seat
and said, "Try again." She didn't
see what good it would do, but he
could see what she couldn't—a
girl on two wheels, her head held
high, a confident smile on her
face. God can see what's ahead
and keep us from falling. And he
can bring us into his presence
without a scratch.

A Moment with God

If you've fallen on
difficult times, trust
God to help you ride
safely through them.
Don't worry, he
won't let go.

For Further Reading:
Jude 1:20-25

Home Is Where the Heart Is

*Revelation 3:20—
Look, I'm standing
at the door and
knocking. If anyone
listens to my voice
and opens the door,
I'll come in and
we'll eat together.*

A Moment with God

Thank God that he shares his presence with you.

*For Further Reading:
Revelation 3:14-22*

*I*magine arriving home on Christmas Eve just after dark. You load your arms with multi-colored boxes clad in ribbons and over-sized bows and step up to the front door. Through the window, illumined by the soft glow of the fireplace, you see family and friends gathered together. You eagerly knock on the door, just waiting for the doorknob to turn. Christmas can bring wonderful memories. But Christmas is more than just a time for presents and fancy dinners. It's a time to celebrate God's gift of becoming a human. Concentrate on the real meaning of Christmas as you celebrate with family or friends. Remember that because of Christmas, God doesn't live in a house, a building, or a church. He lives in the hearts of his people.

Worthy of Our Worship

J ohn gives us a picture of our ultimate destination—standing before God's throne. In the middle of this dazzling setting, 24 rulers are bowing before the living God and saying aloud the attributes of his greatness.

How can you describe the greatness of God who created a universe that spans a hundred million light years and who also designed the delicate body of newborn baby? When we recognize the power and brilliance of God, we can only bow before him in awe. When we arrive in heaven, we will stand in God's presence, overwhelmed by the realization that this great God humbled himself and took the form of a human baby to be born on this day we call Christmas.

DECEMBER 25

Revelation 4:11—"Our Lord and God, you deserve to receive glory, honor, and power because you created everything. Everything came into existence and was created because of your will."

A Moment with God

What attributes of God will you list in your praises when you bow before him in heaven? Practice saying your praises to God today.

For Further Reading: Revelation 4:1-11

359

Always the Center of Attention

Revelation 7:11—All the angels stood around the throne with the leaders and the four living creatures. They bowed in front of the throne with their faces touching the ground, worshiped God.

A Moment with God

Take time to honor and worship God.

For Further Reading: Revelation 7:1-17

*T*here are many mysteries in John's revelation. But there is a constant thread running through it of the sovereignty and centrality of God. For every mysterious, unexplained reference there are many that are clear. God is the central figure in the life after this one, just as surely as he was the central figure in a stable in Bethlehem. God is main event in eternity, just as he is today. He is real. He is present. He is a ruler. He is to be worshiped. It is his throne around which the secondary characters gather. It is his feet at which crowns of life are placed.

God Will Rule Forever

DECEMBER 27

*Revelation 11:15—
The kingdom of the
world has become
the kingdom of our
Lord and of his
Messiah, and he
will rule as king
forever and ever.*

*T*he humble baby whose birth we just celebrated is really the King of the universe, the King of all kings. That means his rule is greater than any other power. It is greater than the combined wisdom, technology, wealth, and resources of all of the superpowers in our world. The Lord's rule is greater than the combined power of all kings and rulers throughout history. He rules in majesty, power, wisdom, and love. Our God reigns, and he reigns forever.

A Moment with God

Praise God, your King, for his glory, honor, power, wisdom, and majesty. Praise him for his love. Allow him to rule your life.

For Further Reading: Revelation 11:11-19

A Devil of a Time

DECEMBER 28

*Revelation 13:5—
The beast was
allowed to speak
arrogant and
insulting things. It
was given authority
to act for 42
months.*

A Moment with God

Thank God that in the end, good will triumph. Praise him that he will one day make heaven your home.

*For Further Reading:
Revelation 13:1-18*

*D*o you ever feel like the world is spinning out of control? How do you deal with gang violence, child pornography, drive-by shootings, serial killings, and other horrible crimes? It seems that things are just going from bad to worse. The devil seems to have control of everything. For a time, perhaps he does. But God will not allow evil to reign forever. He may be patient, but he is still in control. The world is still in his hands. He may allow evil to flourish now, but the time is coming when he will destroy evil and death once and for all. It could be sooner than you think.

The Last
Word

*I*t seems everyone's got an
opinion about God today. But one
day, the truth's coming out in a
spectacular show of splendor. And
all the opinions of people will melt
into awesome wonder before the
holy God of heaven and earth.
Even those who ignored him as a
fable or defiantly rebelled against
his word as a threat to their self-
concept will fall in fearful praise
before his throne and proclaim
with us the truth of the ages: He
is Lord, he is holy, he is the only
true God.

DECEMBER 29

*Revelation 15:4—
Lord, who won't
fear and praise
your name? You
are the only holy
one, and all the
nations will come
to worship you
because they know
about your fair
judgments.*

A Moment
with God
There's coming a day
when what you've
believed will be right
before your eyes.
Keep your praises
strong and exercised.

*For Further Reading:
Revelation 15:1-8*

Rewards for the Heroes

*Revelation 20:6—
Blessed and holy
are those who are
included the first
time that people
come back to life.
The second death
has no power over
them. They will
continue to be
priests of God and
Christ. They will
rule with him for
1,000 years.*

A Moment with God

Praise God for his
faithfulness. He
rewards those who
give their lives
standing for
righteousness
against the forces
of evil.

*For Further Reading:
Revelation 20:1-6*

As God unfolds the final days of
this world, he gives special
attention to the people who were
beheaded because of their
testimony for Jesus and the Word
of God. In God's plan, these
people are the first to be brought
back to life and given positions
serving Christ.

God rewards those who have
been faithful to him. Whatever
pain and suffering they endured
is important to God. The promises of God are fulfilled during
the last days when those who
suffered are given a new life that
will last forever. God is faithful
and loyal to those who have
given everything in their obedience and service. God grants a
greater eternal reward than
anyone could ever obtain during
his or her first life on earth.

Do You Want to Start Over Again?

God is in the business of starting things over. His mercies are new every morning. His sacrifice wipes clean a heart of sin. His love gives second chances to all who believe. And one day, he will wipe the world sparkling clean and allow us to start over. God seems never to run out of new beginnings. He seems never to tire of giving them away. He, in his greatness, is always up for the next leg in the faith journey of one of his children.

DECEMBER 31

Revelation 21:5— The one sitting on the throne said, "I am making everything new." He said, "Write this: 'These words are faithful and true.' "

A Moment with God

The first step to starting over is confessing your sin and asking God for the chance to begin again.

For Further Reading: Revelation 21:1— 22:21

Index